A Music Lover's Art

Wordsongs About
Musical Compositions

A Music Lover's Art

Wordsongs About Musical Compositions

(Fourth Journal In Verse)

MARTIN BIDNEY

Dialogic
Poetry
Press

Song of Dedication:
Happy Thanksgiving
to Roger Brooks, Andre Haykal, Michael Leonard
from Martin

I've eighteen minutes left until the cab arrives
To take me to Thanksgiving with a group of friends.
Well, that's the kabbalistic number "LIFE" and lends
An aid to one who, glad, with lyric vigor strives

To sing deep thanks for what you all have done and do
In greatly helping me be read and heard and seen:
A singer's mood becomes more merry, more serene,
More eager for the future, prospect bright to view.

Your cordial kindness you have blent with crafter-skill,
Ideas to suggest and labor-faith instill.
I know that with your help more people I will reach

(For whom my offerings mayhap might needs fulfil)
By music instrument of shapen lyric speech.
With grateful warmth would I dispel November chill!

11/28/19

Contents

Foreword

═══════════

If you're attracted to classical music, and to intricately crafted euphonious poetry, this may be the book for you. From 5/3/19 to 9/5/19—four months' worth of sheer pleasure—I journaled my reactions to 100 compositions, each by a different composer, and in a few of the poetic "replies" I responded to national or ethnic folk music traditions. I love music—both in tones and in words—with all my heart, with all my soul, and with all my might.

That's why, looking over my 15 years of files since retoolment (let us never speak of retiring), I more than doubled the length and fullness of the book by adding poems on the same composers dealt with in the 100 poems of the main text. The notes introducing the added selections tell you about my musical life, and about the special roles that certain compositions played in it.

I'm a classical violinist and folk fiddler in several traditions, a folk singer in several languages, and a classical chorister—but I was also a university teacher of English and Comparative Literature for 35 years. During that time, I thought a good deal about the relation between music and "wordsong"—my name for musically written poetry, with regularly recurring, often highly original rhythms or "meters," and with not only end-rhymes but patterns of harmony between repeated vowels and between reappearing consonants.

Wordsong has been traditionally called "lyric" verse, meant to be sung to the accompaniment of a lyre or harp (or lute, guitar, dulcimer, psaltery, accordion, harmonium, harpsichord, or piano). I've dramatized the lyrical—or lyre-emulating—function of my verses by reciting them while playing the violin. To hear me sing four of my wordsongs to tunes I composed after I had written the poems, click the link to Episode 8 of my podcast series on website martinbidney. org. To hear fourteen of these, click the website's link to video collage AmericanReal Cycle 6. Both items are also readily available on YouTube.

Bringing together musical wordsong with musical composition, I provide a rhythm chart at the top of each of my 100 musical poems about music. A slash (/) means a STRONG or EMPHASIZED syllable, while an *(x)* indicates a weak syllable, one that's not hit hard in the pronunciation. "MA-ry HAD a LIT-tle LAMB" will be diagrammed "/x /x /x /." In addition, I will sometimes call attention to unusual features of a pervasive rhyme pattern by describing them as part of the informative material right under the poem's title.

The structuring of melodious poems with rhythm structure patterns made of units consisting of strong and weak syllables has been the most prominent feature of poetic tradition in English for the last eight centuries. But some of the forms I use—ancient and modern—deserve to be revived, saved from impending extinction. In my *Bliss in Triple Rhythm—a Toolbox for Poets* I offer nearly 300 poems to show what nine of my favorite rhythmic patterns can give you. In fact, every verse collection I write amounts to a "toolbox for poets."

If you read aloud the poems I present in this book, the "high" of the recitation will surprise you. Vocal performance comes first. After you've become accustomed to it, you may start to hear a voice within your mind reciting the lines you read, so you might not need to continue the readings aloud (yet you still may want to!). Moving your lips, though, is always a great idea. These suggestions of mine are ways of increasing your pleasure.

The variety of my verse forms will show you how I've crafted wordsongs to be as diverse in rhythmic appeal as the music they depict, or evoke. And that fact introduces a topic so huge in implication that it merits a paragraph to itself.

I refer to the miracle presented by the fact that your computer lets you write on your keyboard while you listen to music from your CD! That makes you, the poet, into a sportscaster or game commentator. You're "following the action" on the musical "field" and telling your hearers about it—or, more accurately, singing about it in a wordsong—right while the sport or music event is happening.

It's a transporting feeling, to be able to do this. I did it many times—for Gustav Mahler's "Song of the Earth," for Édouard Lalo's "Symphonie Espagnole," for Alberto Ginastera's piano sonata, for Alexander Glazunov's violin concerto.... My CD with a 32-part theme-and-variations by Dietrich Buxtehude had an individual track for each part of the composition. How did I organize my poem? I paused the computer 32 times, and while listening in this step-by-step way I wrote a 36-line poem in "dactylic distichs."

These last two words come from ancient Greek but have clear and simple modern meanings. A "dactyl" is a three-syllable pattern of "STRONG-weak-weak." And "distich" [DIS-tick] means "two-liner" or "couplet." A dactylic distich is a two-line verse unit made out of dactyls. This is so far from rocket science that a four-year-old child can grasp it with no effort. I can hear the child saying, "LA-la-la, LA-la-la, LA-la-la..." I hope everyone has a good time with these poems—all I want is to share what I love best. The process of making each wordsong was loved with all my heart, with all my soul, and with all my might.

A Music Lover's Art

Wordsongs About Musical Compositions

1 Rameau

Jean-Philippe Rameau (1683–1754),
Complete Works for Harpsichord,
CRD records, 1998, CD 2

Iambic hexameter [= six iambs per line]
x/ x/ x/ x/ x/ x/

We know the allemande, courante, and then perhaps
A minuet, slow sarabande, quick jig to end—
In Bach or Handel suite. The dance plan overlaps,
In Jean-Philippe Rameau, with painting! He'll extend

The music-writing to convey a comic scene:
A flapping, squawking, darting hen we may behold.
Three ladies, agitated, timid, then serene
In triumph next we're watching: genre portraits bold.

In alexandrine sixes I'd an homage frame,
The Gallic elegance to laud and emulate:
A gladsome evening have we passed in classic France.

No telling what Rameau's attention next might claim...
"Lousiana natives" fight—about their fate
We more might wish to learn—they rather seem to
    dance...

5/31/19

2 Moszkowski

Moritz Moszkowski, (1854–1925),
Piano Music,
Helios, Seta Tanyel

*Dactylic pentameter catalectic [catalexis = absent
syllable(s) from final rhythm unit in a verse line]
/xx /xx /xx /xx /*

Floating and flowing and billow and swell—should the
    name
Lent to the melody summon the scene of a dance
(Air de ballet, tarantella, the waltz, minuet)—
Maybe a mood or emotion the minute will claim

(Reverie, twilight, or nocturne, or autumn)—the same
Current or surging or fluttering whirl can entrance
Movement through air and in water a stream to beget
Which in the dimness will memory gentle enflame.

Gliding in gondola, rocked by the wave I recall
Playing the bárcarolle, here for piano transcribed,
We in the orchestra loving the strum and the lull.

Then, to conclude the recital, the opera hall
Fills with bohemian dazzle; excitement, imbibed
Quickly from *Carmen*, no age will avail to annul.

6/2/19

3 Prokofiev

Sergei Prokofiev (1891–1953),
Sonata for Two Violins in C major, op. 56,
Emerson String Quartet, Deutsche Grammophon,
movements 1 and 3

fourth asclepiadic [an ancient Greco-Roman metric form]
  /x /x x/ x/
/x /x x/   /x x/ x/
  /x /x x/ x/
/x /x x/   /x x/ x/

Each impassioned, they joy and grieve,
Let the feelings begun move to their fated end,
    Hope and dream as the years bereave:
Three the roads they will take, each to a height ascend.

Age will come and the lives they wrote,
Neither voice to be dimmed, both in their vigor keen,
    Dancelike rhythms attain and float,
As in ballad of old, valley through mist-veil seen.

Concords then will emerge that were
Never known in their youth, troubled with cries and
    fright:
    Final harmony gods prefer
Hangs irresolute, faint, loved in a higher light.

6/4/19

4 Scarlatti

Domenico Scarlatti (1685–1757)
Sonata K 208, Adagio e cantabile,
in the (555) Complete Keyboard Sonatas,
Scott Ross, harpsichord, Erato

Iambic hexameter; two-stanza rhyme pattern ABCD,
EFGH
x/ x/ x/ x/ x/ x/

The "happiest," the "slowest" and "most beautiful"
Of all selections played on thirty-four CDs—
Our young performer clearly said (he didn't pause)—
Would be the one whose number I transcribed above.

It is a meditation, with a steady pull:
A left-hand chord each four-beat bar begins. With ease
The right hand offers homophonic thought. The laws
Of mood evolving limn a day of work and love.

The pattern is to take a melody motif
And vary it in repetition, as accords
With altered harmony. Arpeggios will do:
The implications, unpredicted, will unfold.

All casual, it yet assumes a firm belief
That what appeared just warm-up will some hid
        rewards
Accumulate. You take a phrase—you think it through...
A story—major, minor—shortly will be told.

We've something like an étude, or an exercise:
You watch what's going on—the sun, the wind, the
    shade—
The first-half weather's brighter; later, care sets in;
But outlines of a tune more clearly will be shown.

Deep liking for a structure means we'll improvise
Yet know while doing it that we'll indeed have made
A worthy statement. The conviction will begin:
To depths we testify that only thus are known.

6/5/19

5 Evening Robin

F. Schuyler Matthews, Field Book of Wild Birds and
Their Music
(New York and London: Putnam's, 1909), p. 250,
as Guide to a Performance of Robins in the Yard

Ovidian dactylic distichs [called Ovidian because
Roman poet Ovid made them popular]
/ xx / xx / xx / xx / xx / x
/ xx / xx /   / xx / xx /

Cheerily! greets you. And also *Cheer UP!* From the
      highest to lowest
   Tone in the call of a bird, rightly transcribed on the
      page,
Barely a fifth is the interval spanned by the song. Yet
      within it,
   Units of two notes or three alternate. Varied, the
      tune.

Range A to E is quite accurate, too. But the Matthews
      performer
   Sounds, when a triad arrives—gladsome—the
      major C sharp.
I would have said the progression more often is heard
      in the minor—
   Yet is the brightness of tone joyful, whatever the
      mode!

Shapes of brief greetings might change, yet the
     structure of each will be steady.
   Think of a bar of four beats. Phrasing quite
     songlike will feel.
What is the total effect on the hearer, by heaven so
     favored?
   Daily more pleasure I gain. Widening smile of a
     friend

Can, in a parallel way, make familiar—a family
     member—
   One who before had been called merely a colleague
     at best.
Robin and I are the artist and hearkener paying an
     homage:
   Tree of the Life of an art, Tree of our Knowledge—
     they're one.

6/5/19

6 Couperin

François Couperin (1668–1733),
Premier Livre de pièces de clavecin, Premier Ordre
(suite of sixteen dances), on disc 1 of 10,
Olivier Baumont, harpsichord, Erato

Iambic hexameters and trimeter
x/ x/ x/ x/ x/ x/
*   x/ x/ x/*
x/ x/ x/ x/ x/ x/
x/ x/ x/ x/ x/ x/

Suppose the robin calls I wrote about last night
        Were labeled "ornaments"
And used to introduce the keyboard notes, made bright
With rapid sparkle-gems—you then would get a sense

Of what the suite I heard today has done. They're swift,
        Enliven mind and nerve—
These two- and three-note stimulators give a lift
To any of our changing moods, with quirk and verve.

The vigor-sprightly things Charlene and I had played
        (On fiddle, keyboard) were
A perfect counterpart to what is here portrayed—
Our Scottish tactics with the Gallic skill concur.

Here, too, the tunes contrast in personality:
        A jig, "La Milordine"
(A wife or daughter of "milord" she seems to be),
Is filled with smiling glee—a dancing Maypole Queen.

But "Les Silvains" a rougher bunch appear to me...
          And people may converse:
A question might we hear—replying speedily,
The answer's entertaining, witty, quick, and terse.

6/6/19

7 Rhetorical Melody

a sentence fragment taken from
Joseph Leo Koerner,
Bosch and Bruegel: From Enemy Painting
to Everyday Life
(Oxford/Princeton, Bollingen Series 37, 2016), p. 264

Trochaic octameter catalectic
/x /x /x /x /x /x /x /

"Let a minor Flemish painter, Joos van Craesbeeck,
    represent…"
[All our struggle now resolving—he'll suggest what
    Bosch had meant.]
Like Hieronymus's Tree-Man in the Garden of Delight,
Mad self-portraiture may castigate our phantasmatic
    sight.

While the open-bottomed monster views the mind-
    unsettling life
That descending from his broken egg-like body love
    and strife
Will continue as it did before, the latter portraiture
Shows a devil mouth and opened skull exuding
    thought impure.

Note the words that I have cited: what they'd clearly
    wish to do
Is convince me, very gently, that the writer's claim is
    true.

His protreptical intention he would never dream to
    hide;
In the words, "Let A mean B," what has the teacher,
    wise, implied?

Fine, persuasive mentor—that's our author, telling how
    things are.
Eight-beat trochees—with a catalexis—carry us quite
    far
From the prosy world of fact to realms where melody
    abides…
He's an apt and keen convincer—*and* with singing skill
    besides!

It is good, when writing prose, to have a rhythm-feel,
    which may
Show a salutary skill at putting metric verve in play.
In a Latin speech, when Tully would the heart of
    hearers move,
He would use dactylic rhythm—and melodic prowess
    prove.

6/7/19

8 Tchaikovsky

Peter Ilyitch Tchaikovsky (1840–1893),
"Iskhodíla Mladyénka," song 1
Fifty Russian Folk Songs (piano, four hands)
CD 8 of 10, Works Without Opus Numbers,
Complete Works for Solo Piano,
Valentina Lisitsa and Alexei Kuznetsoff, Decca

*Anapestic pentameter with alternating feminine and
masculine line endings*
xx/ xx/ xx/ xx/ xx/x
xx/ xx/ xx/ xx/ xx/
xx/ xx/ xx/ xx/ xx/x
xx/ xx/ xx/ xx/ xx/

Iskhodíla Mladyénka—she early went out, friendly
    maiden—
And for thirty-four seconds we listen, and then she is
    gone.
I could tell that her breath in the springtime with
    feeling was laden,
And I wanted to hear what she said while she walked
    on the lawn.

Only two are the phrases—and seven bars each,
    unrepeated.
And the tune is in three, but the first beat's a rest, and
    for me
It was hard to establish the meter. Attempts were
    defeated

Till I played it more times, and the scheme was
    delighted to see.

The tonality? Well, Mixolydian mode. To create it,
We'll establish a base. Though each phrase will
    conclude on a D,
And the F's are all sharp, yet the C's are all natural.
    Mate it
With a major or minor? We can't. Something else it
    must be.

It belongs to the style of a time when the major and
    minor
Hadn't yet settled out from the forms (now "archaic")
    employed
In the structuring used for the hymns in the Church.
    They are finer,
Many times, the creations that earlier ages enjoyed!

The predominant intervals—fourth and a fifth—which
    you're hearing
In the liturgy, still, of the Orthodox Church may be
    heard.
So the maiden whose portrait we view while she walks
    in a clearing
A response may evoke as to Eastern liturgical Word.

You are kept on alert while you listen. For less than a
    minute
Will a song that you pick from the fifty most likely
    endure.

It may end on the dominant, not on the tonic... Within
    it,
Something once-in-a-lifetime goes by. It is perfect, and
    pure.

6/8/19

9 Glazunov

Alexander Glazunov (1865–1936),
Violin Concerto in A minor, Op. 82
Rachel Barton Pine, with Russian National Orchestra,
José Serebrier, Conductor, Warner Classics

Iambic hexameters, trimeter, tetrameter
x/ x/ x/ x/ x/ x/
x/ x/ x/ x/ x/ x/
*   x/ x/ x/*
*   x/ x/ x/ x/*

I heard it when a boy—dreamed happily that night...
And so with hot suspense the youth-mind listened
    hard.
            Postponed—the great delight...
        A looking-backward theme, unmarred

By overactive expectation, geared the will
To follow all the clever metamorphoses
            With which the work would fill
        Twi-mindedly half-wakened reveries.

That wistful opener three times came duly back
In movements one and two and three, as if to hint
            The thinker knew a lack—
        A dullness, reft of solar glint.

Then—crashingly—it happened—Daybreak heavens
    clove!

That folk-like melody I needed to re-love
        No more in hiding strove,
      But trumpet-summoned from above.

The joy-crazed violin with blazing glory flamed
And Praise recalled to life, with grace and light
    endowed:
        O chosen, Angel-named,
      Into the Lord's embrace allowed!

6/8/19

10 Telemann

Georg Philipp Telemann (1682–1767),
Scherzi Metodichi (Pyrmonter Kurwoche), CD 29 of 50,
Violin, viola, violone, harpsichord,
Brilliant Classics

*Dactylic trimeter with double catalexis [= 2 missing
syllables at line-end]*
/xx /xx /

What are "methodical jokes"?
Jollity-week of the suites,
Great entertainment for folks
Here at the spa for some treats.

Dancing in four and in three
(Once he tried six), they had soared
High in the mind while, for me,
Four days of suite-ing outpoured.

Yes, I will finish the rest:
Mood they have "daily" upraised,
Monday through Thursday the test
Aceing, with wit that amazed.

Seven, the tunes in a suite;
Thus, twenty-eight have I scored—
Oddly methodical feat;
Never was anyone bored:

Country-style drone for musette,
Strange hemiolas well made,
Rhythm-types cleverly set
Comic surprise to unlade.

In an American school
Kids would be charmed by the cheer,
Lively Terpsichorë's rule
Nicely designed to endear.

6/9/19

11 Ysaÿe

Eugène Ysaÿe (1858–1931)
Sonata No. 1, dedicated to Joseph Szigeti
Six Sonatas for Solo Violin, op. 27
Tianwa Yang, Deutschland Radio Kultur, Naxos

Alcaic [= Greco-Roman stanza form]
x/ x/ x/ xx/ x/
x/ x/ x/ xx/ x/
  x/ x/ x/ x/x
 /xx /xx /x /x

G minor: brooding, slow, of majestic weight,
The prototype of Bach is the motive strength:
        But plenty of surprises happen—
        Rustle—of leaves—with the bow a-tremble...

The three- and four-note chords will a solemn-deep
And consequential testament-type of thought
        Resume in mood of resolution:
        Rocking arpeggios mull things over.

Two voices in the mind may perspectives trade,
Well moderated till, after careful speech,
        They find a common affirmation,
        Jubilant now in a hymn of triumph.

Both lyrical and whimsical, teenage years
Bring tremor, flutter, hope in the lovers' dream:
        The ending—what a sweet ascension—
        Yet with the spookiest fading timbre.

O heavy peasant tread of the Bruegel shoes!—
I love the go-and-get-'em, the country stomp.
      Quick interludes' amusing travel
    Showed that the whirling affirmed a springtime.

6/11/19

12 Shostakovitch

Dmitri Shostakovitch (1906–1975)
Preludes and Fugues, Op. 87: Nos. 1–8, 12–14
played by the composer, recorded 1952
Revelation Records Ltd.

Hendecasyllabic [= eleven syllables]
/x /xx /x /x /x

1–2

Meditation in form of stately dancing:
Prelude Opener—triple dotted rhythms.
Hinted shadow, Corelli's "La Folía"
Comes to mind, that I used to play when younger.
(Fugue—the opening, tranquil variation.)
Peaceful prelude, and contrapuntal gallop.

3–4

Banter: dare to be crazy-happy, frantic!
Both the freer and stricter forms are frenzied.
Quiet, now, and prepare for contemplation:
Sober, we will explore an olden saying.
Next, another will come to mind, arousing
Unexpected debate, and new excitement.

5–6

Gentle rain is beginning, birds are hopping,
Children fugally splashing in the puddles.

Overture—a surprise—hear gravely striding:
Multi-vocal, the talk is animated—
Then, recalling the pensive mood preceding,
Settles into a calm evaluation.

7–8

Prelude—made in a fit of smiling whimsy,
Sunlight, laughter, and springtime glad to greet us.
Wind-breath alters the key for just a moment...
Fugue is filled with a beaming satisfaction.
Prelude's jubilant, yes—but oh! get ready:
Shared concern will the comrades four consider.

12

Three-beat bars of the weighty passacaglia
Bring to heart the Chaconne of Bach—that marvel!
Solemn turns of a Sufi slowly whirling,
Measured, meaning in every mystic moment.
Ah! the fives of the fugue defy convention:
Sufi attitude well-expressed in humor.

13

Sudden trebles in triumph mock a thoughtful
Concentration that age has brought the Elder;
Yet the two of them soon will sing together...
Youth and age in a tempered, pleasant union
Highlight words I imagine might be fashioned
Heart-wise, planned for the colloquy that follows.

14

Bell-like, single oneiric tones that waken
Cannot quell the unease of steady trembling:
Stymied, baffled, the quester well may ponder
Queries needing a polyphonic treatment.
No reply will appear—but winds of autumn
Dance the branches in many-fulcrum'd balance.

6/15/19

13 Ives

Charles Ives (1874–1954)
Orchestral Music, James Sinclair,
Orchestra New England
Koch International Classics

*Sapphic [one of the most melodious of Greco-Roman
metric forms]*
/ x / x / xx / x / x
/ x / x / xx / x / x
/ x / x / xx / x / x
      / xx / x

Eighteen-nineties, writing your "Ragtime Dances,"
Make them wild, the beats and the beast unloosen—
Chaos-game the same will remain as when you
        "Country Band" followed.

Nor will hymns abandon your dream-flow, ever!
Patriotic marches and praise and rag-tag
Link in snippets fainter and yet forever:
        Sudden, when triumph,

Shouting outburst, cry, or a desperation—
All the types of energy and of trial—
Seem to reach the limit of strength and storming,
        Then—for Elijah—

All is still but—doubting—a half-hid murmur
Pondering, astray in a cloudy chord-land...

Something's broken through—we suppose—a token,
       Then it is fading.

Can you summon back the "Unanswered Question"?
Trumpet, troubled, asked—and, ignored, continued.
Strings, narcissal-blissed, wouldn't turn aside to
       Note the intruder.

"In the Night": a low clarinet will mutter,
Then a cello doubles the long misgiving—
Yet the rumbling thunder, with discord bell-glints,
       Roars—oh, relentless.

Ives a comment offered: an old man's thinking;
Everything had vanished but "faith" and "mem'ries."
Cello, clarinet—he will chant till dying.
       No one need hear him.

14 Bidney

Martin Bidney (1943–)
Fourteen Songs in Ancient Classical Strophes
[Greek for "Stanzas"]
to poems written by Bidney and Philipp Restetzki
(translated by Bidney)
sung in episodes of Live Tribe 21,
on AmericanReal video collage Martin Bidney Cycle 7,
and on The Be-Loving Imaginer Podcast 8 (YouTube)

Third asclepiadic [Philipp's favorite Greco-Roman stanza form]
/ x / xx / / xx / x /
/ x / xx / / xx / x /
*   / x / xx / x*
*   / x / xx / x /*

No, I couldn't have dreamt... What?! A composer?—me?
Yet the song-writer call, summoning, made a claim—
            Hidden mission discloser—
      Music Writer, your newest Name!

Source? Bilingual, the tome: colloquy, age and youth.
Total? Seventy-five lyrics in e-mails writ.
            Changing station and stage and
      Feeling-truth was the aim of it.

Every stanza we shaped using an olden frame,
Rhythms picked from the ones Grecian and Roman
      wrote.

       Genius great let embolden
    Modern sailors in ancient boat!

One more space will await, ere I the *Kreis* may close
With the number required, total, of episodes...
       Violin will arise! May
    Fiddle music adorn our odes!

6/20/19

15 Copland

Aaron Copland (1900–1990)
"The Quiet City," on first disc of two,
Hugo Wolff, The Saint Paul Chamber Orchestra, Teldec

Iambic heptameters and hexameters in opening strophe
x/ x/ x/ x/ x/ x/ x/
x/ x/ x/ x/ x/ x/ x/
*   x/ x/ x/ x/ x/ x/*
*   x/ x/ x/ x/ x/ x/*
Iambic heptameters, hexameters, and pentameters
variously patterned

The trumpet has reopened the discussion Ives began.
How "quiet" will the "city" be? The strings have listened
        in
    As they had done before, yet here an answer can—
    We sense—in pensive windbreath barely stirred—
        begin...

    The tension builds, 'mid muffled hints of a reply.
    The rooftop questioner declaims relentless. Comes
    A reassuring nod from cello: roused am I...
    He raised from where they slept his child-time
        halidoms.

        A dialogue will start with strings that reach
        A height of curiosity, concern.
        Then—pause. New life the night may teach
        And in a strange direction mind might turn.

A dancelike dotted theme, alert, in triple beat,
  Had slowed to marching rhythm. Striding
    strong,
  The two and three in balance—we can greet
The trumpeter who'll reaffirm the starting song.

Reply has not arrived. Resolve had made its way
In wakeful contemplation ere the sleep with might
Of tiredness overcame it. Comes the break of day,
We rise refreshed by what occurred and know it's
    right.

6/21/19

16 Schubert

Franz Schubert (1797–1828)
Sonata in B flat, D 960, first movement, Molto moderato
Alfred Brendel, piano, disc 2 of 2, Philips

Iambic hexameters in opening strophe
x/ x/ x/ x/ x/ x/
Iambic pentameters and hexameters variously patterned
x/ x/ x/ x/ x/

The nearly hymn-like song adversity beheld,
First lyric phrase encountering a thunder's roar.
The second try will show the foe he met before...

New tune, another key? Mood quietens awhile
But only when the melody with roar can meld.
A triplet wind now comes, more friendly to the style
Of springtime stroll—that, tripping, turns to lither
    dance.

The moods of calm and storm are passing back and
    forth:
A trace of thunder-threat in minor will enhance
The shrewd elaborated turns the twain will take,
Winds kindly intertwining from the south and north.

    But—after what had proved too long a break—
    The rumbling's back. New theme? 'Tis yet too
        weak.
We'll test again our opening—rethink, and seek

A treaty, major-minor blent, as dance with roar,
    A triplet-grace portrayed with louder pride
    Assumed in trying out a marching stride.

Accompanying dark yields way. No thunder-pour—
Subdued all impulse, and the dancing, dreamlike
            made,
    Slowed down. The spring-motif—loved all the more.
The storm may threaten yet, but rain should be
            delayed.

6/23/19

17 Cowell

Henry Cowell (1897–1965)
Homage to Iran
Continuum Ensemble
Instrumental, Chamber and Vocal Music 2, Naxos

Iambic pentameters and hexameter in opening strophe
*   x/ x/ x/ x/ x/*
x/ x/ x/ x/ x/ x/
*   x/ x/ x/ x/ x/*
Iambic pentameters and hexameters variously
patterned, feminine line endings in second strophe

Lord of the Dawn, the giant drum awakes
The little tabrets and the sleepy violin,
    Which latter puts in order many thoughts...

Another summoning alarm of Daybreak
Enlivens further, strengthened speculative effort,
    Applauded by the drumming when it pauses.

Augmented seconds— trilling non-adjacent notes—
Grown quiet, fading out, piano comes to aid
The fiddle, bowed and pizzicato—what the west
Would call a tarantella—fevered, freshened, quick.

The chant, continuing in Part the Third,
A story-telling, may fulfil a deep-known need
    Though wordless: morning-time society.

The fiddle starts a flaring dance of dare;
And, thundering, the drummer's getting strange...
A nine-eight gallop—rests, to catch your breath!—
We're singing while we dance. Piano helps:

A drone, a drum, a triumph cry, an end.

6/24/19

18 Schoenberg

Arnold Schoenberg (1874–1951)
Concerto for String Quartet and Orchestra in B flat
after the Concerto Grosso Op. 6 No. 7 by George
Frideric Handel
The Fred Sherry String Quartet, Twentieth Century
Classics Ensemble
The Robert Craft Collection: The Music of Arnold
Schoenberg, vol. 2
Naxos

Iambic heptameter in opening line
x/ x/ x/ x/ x/ x/ x/
Iambic heptameters, hexameters, tetrameters variously
patterned

Concerto grosso reinvented, high school days for me
Return when I the Handel work delighted had
   performed.
     The hymning overture most bold though brief will
       be
     Before the sequent fugue. Polyphonies have
       swarmed
     Through registers and timbres, interrupted first
       With rumination, next with loudenings,
And finally with playful tease. The brave quartet
Concludes with whimsy.
        Tender prayer? Yes, I think…
(I don't remember that from Handel.) We are set
To rest awhile by soothing lull of sleepy strings.

Third movement melody will, plénipotent, link
      My memories in mirthful burst:
Crazed muted wanderings of prankish violins
Converse with warnings that the orchestra will
    make.
        But wait—the foursome dream awhile—
    More dialogue—quartet in reverie
Requires harmonic explorations tricky to attain...
      Yet suddenly new bliss we gain:
The mustering rumbustious hornpipe will awake
    The full potential of what now begins
    A great parade in every kind of style.
First violin will try for leadership, I guess,
But solos and ripieno in their rivalry-largesse
    Ignore the calls to order from the kettle drums
      Till fading coda, quiet, comes.

6/24/19

19 Hindemith

Paul Hindemith (1895–1983)
Concerto for Orchestra Op. 38
Berlin Philharmonic, disc 1 of 3
Hindemith Conducts Hindemith:
The Complete Recordings on Deutsche Grammophon

Ovidian dactylic hexameter distichs
/ xx / xx / xx / xx / xx / x
/ xx / xx /   / xx / xx /

"Schnell Number 5" was our junior high humor. The
        "Eight Easy Pieces"
    Proved you could "travel" your tune, sailing
        through several keys.
Striking motif I am singing right now: happy whimsy
        releases
    Double the joy of that time—wit will the intellect
        please.

Strong is the memory, giving the listener brain-
        motivation:
    Yes, we two guys are alike, firmly baroque in our
        taste.
Wistful he often will be, with a doldrum, a megrim.
        Elation
    Sudden may burst through the door, drunk, with
        importunate haste.

Teenage exuberance, Bachian Brandenburg
    counterpoint-thinking:
  Oboe, bassoon, violin—colorful soloist group.
Tossing the theme to and fro, how capricious the
    rising, the sinking:
  Mad are the winds that compete, swaying the
    schooner, the sloop.

Wait, there's no break—don't you dare to expect what
    you'd call a conclusion!
  Rather, a storm breaking through—crazing the
    birds in the air.
Swift and impulsive, 'twas gone. Then a groundbass
    came stately... Confusion
  Has to return, though: the winds wander in
    reveries rare.

Look what showed up—the continuo, unison! Yet in a
    minute
  Here's a new tempo for dance—wildly the bird-
    flights begin.
Jig is the victory project with bliss-of-community in it.
  Dissonance comes but to go: lyrical spirit, you win.

6/27/19

20 Foster

Stephen Foster (1826–1864)
"Oh, Willie, Is It You, Dear?"
Stephen Foster Songs
John Van Buskirk, Ridley Enslow, Steve Schneider,
and others
Albany Records US / UK

But my heart grew sad again, when I found you had not
*   come;*
Oh, Willie, we have missed you—welcome, welcome
*   home.*

Trochaic octameter catalectic
/x /x /x /x /x /x /x /

Every August it would happen, as dependable as warm,
A festivity of music took tradition-hallowed form:
From the glad-illumined stage we heard the hammer,
    pluck, and strum:
For the Gathering of Dulcimers the summer fun had
    come.

'Twas "Hard Times" I chiefly hoped that I would hear
    again that night.
Both for me and for my daughter—favored Foster!—
    more delight
Would be added if a singer picked your fine familiar
    strain
Prized in phrasing and in harmony, annihilating pain.

I have brought it back to mind because I raptly
    listening
To this welcome, overwhelming, never known, began to
    sing.
'Tis ridiculous to weep for this, and yet I want to try
To discover what might make an aging writer start to
    cry.

I was picturing a friendship circle; these, when I
    returned,
Planned to grant to me a present they considered I had
    earned
While so long away in work and travel. Blest who, when
    they roam,
Hear the question, "Is it you, dear?" and the "Welcome,
    welcome home."

6/28/19

21 O'Carolan / Moore

"The Young May Moon"
music by Turloch O'Carolan (1670–1738),
from part "A" of his "Planxty Peyton,"
words by Thomas Moore (1779–1852),
Dear Harp of My Country: The Irish Melodies
of Thomas Moore
by James W. Flannery, performances
by James Flannery, tenor,
and Janet Harbison, Irish Harp, J. S. Sanders & Co.,
Nashville TN
disc 1 song 1

And the best of all ways
To lengthen our days
Is to steal a few hours from the night, my dear.

Iambic, amphibrachic, anapestic tetrameters and
dimeters, with slight variants
  x/x x/ x/ x/
xx/x x/x x/ x/
     xx/ x/
    x/x x/
x/x x/x x/ x/

O'Cárolan's harp resounds for me
And the night in delight abounds for me
    When the lyre I hear
    Revealing the cheer
Which Ireland inspired re-astounds for me.

I'm loving the troubadour lines you made
And, for sweetheart to hear, the designs you made:
  Tom Moore, you've a heart
  That mastered the art
Of rousing the mind with the wines you made.

Dear Flannery, Harbison—voice and strings—
You make me a man who'll rejoice and sings:
  With Carolan, Moore—
  Quartet of the pure,
I join in this heavenly choice of kings.

I want to remember it all my days—
In dream and awake to recall my praise:
  I'll croon it for friends,
  The tune that commends
A soul that with this from the fall I raise.

6/29/19

22 Romanian Folk Music

The Edge of the Forest:
Romanian Music from Transylvania
recorded 1991–1993
compiled by Martha Lorantos and Speranța Rădulescu
Music of the World, Ltd.

hendecasyllabic
/x /xx /x /x /x

Transylvanian Jamfest—many hamlets'
Fiddlers kept my attention wakeful, eager.
Double bass and viola, maybe mouth harp,
Kept the beat, from the placid to the frantic:
Tetrachords with a major-minor wedding
Meant the harmonies couldn't be predicted.

When musicians in Binghamton would gather,
I to one or another of their weekly
Sessions frequently went to play for pleasure:
Turf Exchange, or the Java Joe collective...
Here, however, a wholly new idea
Startled, gladly, the traveler in music.

Stellar poet, the fiddler, polestar magnet,
Stroking tones with a glitter-trill resplendent,
Draws the crowd at a tempo reaching frenzy,
Double, triple adornments freely adding:
Flute, or pipe, to accompany the Master
Copies all, with a shared acute precision.

Every dance will a narrative encompass:
Thus I have to conclude—the phrases, lengthened,
Picture, proud, their imagined destination,
Run, or gallop, or skip and—leaping lightly—
Glorifying the story they are telling—
Make me think of Olympic racer legends.

6/30/19

23 Bartók

Muzsikás: The Bartók Album
Béla Bartók (1881–1945)
Muzsikás Vocal and Instrumental Ensemble
Phonographic folk music from the Ethnographic
Museum of Hungary
Hannibal Records

First asclepiadic
/x /xx / /xx /x /

Loud the chirruping birds, vivid and dawning-clear:
Why so many at once, crowding to sing the light?
Sudden—smiling—I knew: these were supporting
   friends.
On the disc they had heard, chanting, an aged man.

Bartók rendered the voice, graced with the choral tones.
He recorded them all—fiddler and drum and flute.
Modern dancing and song, most in the Magyar mode,
Some Rumanian, too (language he tried to learn).

Ethnological tape, cylinder disc—we find
Tunes done often in ways Bartók had reconceived.
Folk-made versions are heard, too, in a shifting stream,
As on Proustian page, memories blent in sound.

Here's a man in a bass register, very low,
Peasant fife at the height, mutual mirrors apt:
Every ornament done, each as the partner did—
Feeling, deep and the same, filling the space between.

Voices mainly I loved—womanly, old or young—
Which the songs would perform known to the fiddler
      brave,
Tried on perilous hike, wild as the blood of youth,
Then, returning to her, words of our life to join!

7/1/19

24 Milhaud

Darius Milhaud (1892–1974)
Music for Wind Instruments
(La Cheminée du roi René and other suites)
Athena Ensemble
Chandos CD

Iambic hexameter
x/ x/ x/ x/ x/ x/
Two-stanza rhyme pattern ABCD, EFGH

The tender green of limpid nimble oboe tone,
Soft blue of clarinet and humor of bassoon,
The flute a crimson hover-bird in summer sun,
Dark purple horn a huntsman loving a parade—

The colors of a ducal Book of Hours are known
For purity and elegance—a rigadoon
In meadow-fresh Provence—loved medieval fun—
Enameled hues on vellum delicately laid.

The suites reveal a cordial friendship with Rameau.
The genre-painting—the jongleur, cortège, aubade,
The nocturne, madrigal, the venery, the hounds—
Were taught indeed by him, who'd equally portray

The forms of courtly dance—the tambourin, rondeau,
The serenade, the fanfare, minuet, ballade;
The satisfaction of a child-surprise abounds—
Rameau's "The Hen" would phrasing for "The Cuckoo"
    play.

The portraiture of mood more kinship illustrates.
We've "Balanced," then "Dramatic," lastly "Gladsome."
    These
Are facial types, or limnings of a character.
We close with madrigal and pastoral, at ease.

The underlying calm of kindly mind elates.
Enlivened by contrasting personalities
And by the wayward chords that wander and bestir—
Enchanting is the blending of the centuries.

7/2/19

25 Piazzolla

Astor Piazzolla (1921–1992)
Bandoneón Concerto
CD Sinfonia Buenos Aires and other works
Daniel Binelli, soloist
Nashville Symphony Orchestra,
Giancarlo Guerrero, conductor
Naxos

Iambic heptameter opening line
x/ x/ x/ x/ x/ x/ x/
Iambic octameters, heptameters, hexameters,
pentameters variously patterned

Bandoneón—(the concertina)—keyboard, strings—
    affirm
A starting strength, a gladness in their speaking-
    life combined:
Relaxing, they together dream. The solo-friend may
    squirm
Awhile in tortured turnings—yet, in cousin-calm
    resigned,

They murmur gently their assent, till he's
        prepared
The tango theme to reassert, which now is
        dared:
    The *one* two three *four* five six *sev'n* eight;
        hear
    The master-dance of all our days made
        clear.

A mournful walk alone, with playful memory is
        punctuated...
A dreamy harp and violin will come to aid; they long
        awaited
    A fitting time to reminisce, evaluate, and plan:
    Your friends in darkness come to light: with vigor
        unabated
    They help you to explore, explain, expand. Ah,
        happy man!

The zany weather alternates the cloud and sun, the
        blue and gray...
                An emblem of our life, the walkers will
                    conclude—
Till suddenly—we don't know why—a heavy rhythm
        intervenes:
    A one *two* three four, one *two* three four, one *two*
        three four—scenes
    Will change, but stolid constancy may cause of
        grief elude.

    Good friends to have who understand is better
        than to pray.

7/3/19

26 Schumann / Debussy

Robert Schumann (1810–1856),
Claude Debussy (1862–1918)
Schumann, 6 Études, Op. 86,
set for 2 pianos by Debussy
CD Debussy, Arrangements for 2 Pianos
Marco Polo, DDD

Amphibrachic pentameter catalectic
x/x x/x x/x x/x x/

Canonic invention, most Bachian, mind to elate,
With dream of mellifluent Schumann is wishing to
    mate.
Some lyrics have come to my lips: do I dare to inscribe
This wine-bringing ardor that melody lovers imbibe?

We, brave, on the waves (with the glare in our eyes)
    take a ride:
Turn 'round—let the barcarolle sound, and the hat-
    brim let hide
Your face: may the blend of the ruddy and paleness
    remain
Protected in shadow, let drops of the water-splash
    rain—

A gust—feel it coming?—propelling our boat, lending
    skill
Our journey to guide with alertness and practical will,

By raising the strength and the tempo, may hint at the
    course
Our thinking might gain unconstrained—oh the fervor,
    the force!

Canonic, the singing takes over—our calls to and fro
Communicate changing ideas of where we may go:
The currents of water—they roar!—and yet turning
    aside
The tiniest bit makes our chanting, unhampered,
    abide.

That Cossack-type dance—quite entrancing—of
    yesterday night,
With leaping and hopping and skipping of maiden and
    wight—
Each crest of a glittering wave will in dazzle recall
The white of the towering hats and the candle-lit hall...

The lavender-mauve in the west, and the mist, and the
    still
Of waters that rest from their wave-whipping wind-
    swelling shrill
Have settled, and hymns from our childhood arising
    beguile:
We answer each other again—then, we're quiet awhile.

7/4/19

27 Sarasate

Pablo de Sarasate (1844–1908)
Zigeunerweisen, in Music for Violin
and Orchestra vol. 1
Tianwa Yang, Orquesta Sinfónica de Navarra,
Conducted by Ernest Martínez Izquierdo
Naxos

Iambic heptameter
x/ x/ x/ x/ x/ x/ x/

We talked of song. The taxi driver hailed from Ecuador.
"On violin, when I was young, I learned to play a tune,
Deep-feeling, sad, and slow, and Spanish. Heart you
   must outpour
And save your bow for what you know will happen,
   though not soon:

Each lengthened phrase a half-a-dozen rapid notes
   would end,
Or—when emotion from a greater depth was coming
   through—
In fit proportion to the strength, these too might then
   extend;
More drama to the stretching-out more pleasure gave
   to you.

Well, want to hear it?" "Sure!" I sang to show what I
   had meant.
The Sarasate Malagueña brought me back to youth.

A single string—the lowest—proved it to the full extent
Back then, and now again I felt the heart-portraying
    truth.

Zigeunerweisen—German term for Gypsy melodies—
Felt blended with the singing and the playing I had
    done.
The grand, majestic flourishing the grown-up soul
    would please:
The orchestra and gloried violinist are at one

In declaration, testament, Flamenco joie de vivre—
The fiddler now will take some time her bag of tricks to
    show:
The left-hand pizzicato, high harmonics—bateau ivre!
Then—holy prayer, thoughtful, and with silences that
    glow!

Finale friska Liszt in his "Hungarian Rhapsody"
Had used, as in the middle movement opera quotes we
    heard.
So Rómany and Magyar helped the Spaniard make for
    me
A riant-blithe inspirer for a blest poetic word.

28 Enescu

Georges Enescu (1881–1955)
Sonata No. 3 in A Minor for Violin and Piano, Op. 25
subtitled "in the Rumanian national character"
The Weilerstein Duo
Arabesque Recordings

Вспрянь, желай, и будь силён! [Leap, desire, be lithe
and strong!]
—Saul Tchnernikhovsky

First asclepiadic
/x /xx / /xx /x /

Final statement to make, look in your dark and write!
Else remaining unknown, pray and it comes to light.
Spirit wailing I hear, groping around in doubt:
Murmured comfort of strum—throwing the demon out?

Sunlight comes—we affirm, song and the dance are
    life.
Strings and keyboard explore: search is a worthy strife.
Couples dreamlike appear, whirling in space—at home,
Lifted now in a field—lit by the sunset gloam.

Barely hearable beat—is it a tabret drum?
All-harmonic the tune—gradual thoughts will come...
Will they? Silence arrives—why? we're obliged to guess:
Batlike wings in the air—Nature—a threat-largesse.

Octaves try to assert: here is a mission found!
Sparkles flash in the sky—holding my breath, no
    sound...
All the dancing I've prized most in my life would seem
Ready, set to return—see! the ideas teem.

Solos trade, and technique—plucking and open
    strings,
Wilder sliding, and chords pound while the fiddle sings.
Many unisons huge—fast, unrelenting, proud—
Burst—mere Time to deride—speak to the world—
    shout loud!

Joy and strength and desire! Cry of the free! despair
Blent with all that's affirmed—so in Hasidic pray'r:
Hark the rumbling below—cloudbanks that more won't
    hold
Roar, exhorting, and pour!—storming! My story—told!

7/6/19

29 Dohnányi

Ernst von Dohnányi (1877–1960)
Sonata for Violin and Piano Op. 21
The Weilerstein Duo, Arabesque Recordings

Iambic heptameter
x/ x/ x/ x/ x/ x/ x/

Another Brahms sonata for the violin? At times
I felt how well the vocal style with mentor-model
  rhymes.
I'd ev'n begin to sing, and—yes!—the major-minor
  switch
Would happen (as directed by the ghost): to wonder
  which
Tonality we're in was something guaranteed to give
Melodic joy to violin—make wander-impulse live.

The fiddle and piano will exhilarations trade:
My friend and I, when playing Brahms, the most had
  always made
Of lyric statement boldly shared, and tossing to and
  fro:
I'm also thinking—Ede Zathureczky once could know
Dohnányi as a friend and colleague. Of my teacher I
Am telling—two Hungarians who sang into the sky.

Professor Zathureczky little English could command,
But there's a phrase—bel canto!—that was always
  right at hand.

I hear him say it while I write—just now the climax
    came
When violin-piano fortress-breaching strength would
    claim!
The two musicians caution me: words only go so far
As hidden Eden-place to hint, where the immortal are.

The second movement, air and variations, had the feel
Of Schubert's canorous-dramatic ballad-lieder. We'll
Be accurate as well if we with equal love recall
The "Gypsy" themes in Brahms' quartet that overpower
    all...
The theme comes back, as if poetic words it would
    request:
A playful pizzicato ending—then it's laid to rest.

The Rómany-Brahms combo turns the bold finale wild:
I'm typing now more swiftly—Make the chanting fiery-
    styled,
Most helpful houri-muse! Indeed, my feet desire to
    dance—
I'd leap and spring and cry in this impassioning
    romance:
The major-minor blend, chromatic entertainment, zest
In ever-graced bel canto... Teacher-pupil union blest.

7/7/19

30 Khachaturian

Aram Khachaturian (1903–1978)
Violin Concerto
Itzhak Perlman, Israel Philharmonic,
Zubin Mehta conducting
EMI Digital

Trochaic hexameter catalectic
/x /x /x /x /x /

Swept and flown along by strong folkloric theme,
Pause, enrapt in song, a soothing, moving dream...
Brief cadenza, quick—then dance and reverie
Blest are melding—to the rising writer-glee.

(Now the fiddler has a relaxation-break,
Let me clarify: a silly tech mistake
Led to the destruction of my disc machine...
So? Computer came to aid! I'm blithe, serene...)

Back to music: middle movement, soft, begins...
Yet with growing tension, pressure. Fiddler wins
Greater breathing space to mull a recent grief:
Lower strings affirm a unison-belief—

Statement violin will vary while he adds
Confirmation. Heads are nodding: sorrow glads
Firm support of friendly thought. The group entire
Backs him up, a loved requital for desire.

Part the Third: we village-freedom celebrate—
Skipping, hopping, leaping, somersaulting... Wait!—
Melody, from nap awaking, soon becomes
Love-hymn tribute, sung to gentle rhythmic thrums.

Violin-gymnastic, acrobatic stunts,
Prove he'll catch the quarry wheresoe'er he hunts...
Now, to country-theme, much loved, when we return,
Variants, new-flourishing, more graces earn.

7/10/19

31 Rossi

Salomone Rossi (1570–1628)
"Adon Olam" ("Lord of the World")
Hashirim asher li'Shlomo (The Songs of Solomon), 2 CDs
Kühn Chamber Soloists, Symposium Musicum
(recorded in Prague)

Iambic tetrameter
x/ x/ x/ x/

I love it best of all the hymns
The loving Hebrew heart produced.
God's holy depth a beauty limns,
Which had a sacred flame unloosed

In Salomone Rossi, who
With triple and quadruple beat
A varied art had brought to view,
For Jewish masterwork most meet.

This hymn in dear Hebraic speech
I daily chanted many years.
I pray my rendering may reach
The soul of one that Heaven hears:

"Eternal Lord, He reigned alone
Before a creature yet was made.
When all had by His will been shown
He was in kingly praise arrayed.

When everything shall end, His reign
Whom we adore, continues. He
That was, and is, will yet remain
In glory and in majesty.

No second. Know the Lord, the One
With Whom none other we compare.
Unending He, and unbegun:
All strength and all dominion fair.

Redemptor, and my living God!
My stronghold in a time distressed,
My guide, my refuge, and my rod,
And, when I call, my goblet blest.

To Him my spirit I commend
Whom I, awake, asleep, revere.
Soul, body, may He blessing lend:
With me stands God. I shall not fear."

7/10/19

32 Bach or Not Bach

Johann Sebastian Bach (1685–1750)
Bach or not Bach: Early Harpsichord Works
Christian Rieger, soloist
Westdeutscher Rundfunk Köln

Iambic octameter in opening strophe
x/ x/ x/ x/ x/ x/ x/ x/
Iambic octameters, heptameters, hexameters variously
patterned

We're all invited—let's partake: a feast it surely may
    appear,
Especially as player skill can deftly make the spirit
    clear.
We're offered what a question raised: the food is good—
    by whom prepared?
We thought it all cooked up by Bach, though doubts
    have been by scholars dared.

Concerto in D major I have many times enjoyed.
D Minor Prelude, Fugue are new, perfection
    unallóyed.
Majestic, B Flat Major Suite: Praeludium is grand;
And stately, what Americans might rhyme as
    "allemande."

Courante will make you race—it runs in jig-
    like threes!
We'll catch our breath in Sarabande and take
    our ease.

Concluding Echo—yes indeed, with every
    phrase
Played louder, then repeated soft and sweet. O
    praise!

G major fugue—a longer subject means a briefer
    piece.
E minor will attempt a kind and tranquil mind-
    release,
Though intellect's in fact required, the wander-path
    to trace.
The final try—E minor—smiles on fugal-humored
    face.

Partita, brave: a gracious allemande to sing,
Then Air for Trumpet! Clarion, your summons
    ring!
Exuberant, exhilarated, we rejoice
Before the sarabande will calm our fevered
    voice.

O speediest bourrée—competitor of Handel's—glad you
    came!
It needs an agile dancer-hand for apter answer to your
    claim;
The jig as well—how masterly—Bach's later jig-fugue
    comes to mind...
But here is something unexpected: improvised, and
    truly wild,
The prelude! and the fugue? exciting, too, for choral
    singing styled.

Cornelius Heinrich Dretzel really wrote it? *That* is what
    you say?
"We never had suspected, till a manuscript that came
    our way
Had proved the case." I love it still, to "facts" am readily
    resigned.

7/11/19

33 Byrd

William Byrd (1543–1623)
First Pavan and Galliard
Glenn Gould Plays Renaissance and Baroque Music,
CD 1 of 2
Glenn Gould, piano
SONY Classical

*First strophe iambic hexameters, two with feminine line
endings, two with masculine*
x/ x/ x/ x/ x/ x/x
x/ x/ x/ x/ x/ x/x
  x/ x/ x/ x/ x/ x/
  x/ x/ x/ x/ x/ x/
*Iambic hexameters follow, with masculine and feminine
line endings variously patterned*

To every note, and pause, and volume alteration
Due heed I pay. The pávan is a conversation.
        Repeated in another register, a phrase
        Will change in feeling-tone, and many other ways.

        The treble and the bass, in shapen melodies,
        Will bring across contrasting personalities.
Canonic galliard-interchange I hear conveying
The traits, attractive, of the men the two are "playing."

        Paired voice-dynamics clearly differ in degree,
        To give their traits of character more subtlety.
Confiding in their tone, each pávan-, galliard-spirit
Is "known," and both "alone" in soul: I see and hear it.

And every uttered note, with loving touch endearing,
Is quite distinctive in its own well-lighted clearing—
    And when a section is repeated, 'twill have proved
    It truly was by wholly new emotion moved.

7/11/19

34 Mendelssohn

Felix Mendelssohn (1809–1847)
Psalm 42, Op. 42, Wie der Hirsch schreit, disc 6 of 6
London Symphony Chorus, Richard Hickox,
Janet Baker, solo
EMI Classics

First strophe amphibrachic pentameter catalectic
x/x x/x x/x x/x x/
Amphibrachic pentameter strophes catalectic variously
patterned with trochaic and iambic tetrameter strophes

The hart after waterbrook panting—O heart, that is I:
For mercy I'm crying—show grace to the chanter you
    hear!—
With clamor of hope, while my arms are upraised, need
    I fear?
Your creatures you guard, night and day, with
    compassionate eye.

    I with crowds had glad proceeded
    To the House of God: their mirth,
    Pray'r of thanks, with tears I heeded—
    Where has't gone, my help on earth?

    My heart for you is thirsting—when
    Will next your pilgrim know your voice?
    I fain would issue from the den
    Of darkness, and in light rejoice...

"O wait for the Lord, and the radiant countenance dear
Will shine through the dark and to plea with a pardon
    reply."
The deep to the deep calling forth, unrelenting, would
    sigh...!
The flood overswept one who summoned. My Friend—is
    he near?

    It comes—the choir. They, praising him,
    Intone as folk bestirred by love:
    Why silent, pray, O friend above?
    Your heaven-face I fain would limn!

"Disquiet, my spirit—I beg you—forget, and be calm.
The vision requested will come—with a bliss
    reattained.
Of Israel the helper eternal, great favor is gained
To whom you will make, with the grace that is given, a
    psalm."

35 Bernstein

Leonard Bernstein (1918–1990)
Clarinet Sonata, transcribed for cello and piano
by Yo-Yo Ma
Yo-Yo Ma and Jeffrey Kahane
CD Made in America, SONY Classical

Alcaic (slightly modified, with feminine rhymes allowed
for lines 1 and 2
x/ x/ x/ xx/ x/(x)
x/ x/ x/ xx/ x/(x)
   x/ x/ x/ x/x
   /xx /xx /x /x

In forty-three, the year I was born, arose
Prophetic-minded, what the composer chose
      To publish—talent, young, awaking:
   Great is the pleasure today we're taking!

How Brahmsian, the warmth of the starting lyric.
The keyboard's rapid rhythm? A panegyric—
      I name it—to the vivid spirit,
   Trademarking Bernstein—we feel and hear it.

The three-four alternation's a rhythmic journey...
Now fiddle and piano in friendly tourney,
      Their lyric, metric roles exchanging,
   Like to surprise me, in time-speed ranging.

We move to meditation and, softly gentle,
A calm is earned. The physical and the mental

Exertions and the sound invention
Well represent a profound intention.

(I'm minded of a Chichester Psalm.) The second,
The andantino movement, to thought has beckoned
    Of where the theme austere may travel—
  Game?—we're amazed: let the calm unravel!

The double-metered rushing, the headlong racing,
More syncopated—ere to a pensive pacing
    We're led, while quiet keyboard-voicing
  Solemnly alters our first rejoicing.

A meditative quest we are undertaking
Until, all structures—tranquil—of wonder shaking,
    On holiday precipitated
  Forward in chaos we're quite elated.

7/12/19

36 Kirchner

Leon Kirchner (1919–2009)
Triptych, cello first and third movements,
piano with cello obbligato in the second
Lynn Chang, Yo-yo Ma
CD Made in America SONY Classical

Iambic hexameter, slightly variable rhyme patterns
x/ x/ x/ x/ x/ x/

We'll ruminate on problems of our troubled mind.
If tensions grow, we pause—intensified may then—
Or somewhat quietened, who knows?—unloose or bind
Conflicted ties in sudden calm, in lighted glen
Or gloomy wood, or—what is that? A beacon-bird?

A violin has come—a wise and feisty friend,
Who can at times be patient, yet we'll soon have heard,
In dialogue replies, what battle can extend
To shared bipolar swing and switching. Next? A word
Of teasing, jocular… They, friendlier, converse:

Arousal follows—no dispute, plain query posed…
Then question-answer list of possibilities.
The violin got frantic when the cello glozed
The outlook in a sanguine fashion, too much ease!
(A football commentator haven't I become?)

The rhythms—they are getting odder!—devildom
Is breaking loose—in therapeutic mode—so now

We hear a trembling chord of peace. Part Three: a
    drum
And banjo are implicit—Presto! can allow
Ecstatic jazz all woe in concord to immerse.

7/13/19

37 Gershwin

George Gershwin (1898–1937)
Three Preludes, arranged by Jascha Heifetz
transcribed for violin and piano by Yo-yo Ma
Yo-yo Ma and Jeffrey Kahane
CD Made in America, SONY Classical

Iambic hexameter
x/ x/ x/ x/ x/ x/

Piano called, awakened; fiddle glad replied:
The beat is *one* two three *four* five six *sev'n* eight—Go!
The Charleston rhythm, tunes will quickly build upon,
While plucking gives the feel of thrum and smiling
    light;
Staccato, double-stopping, gliding, low and high—
A bag of tricks—we love 'em—keep it up—don't stop!

A steady plodding, one and two, and up and down:
The alternating phrase la *la* la, third and fourth,
Will form a lullaby (and Gershwin called it so).
The saddened melody is warmed by pulsing love:
Though life be trouble, yet the child-heart is a joy.
Da capo—softer hymn of suffering and peace.

Your syncopated skit, with semi-drunken clowning—
Get zanier—don't care!—you know how much we like
    it:
Affirm your motto in triumphant celebration—

To sing while leaping 'round the flag-draped stage,
    well-lighted,
Is nothing more than to become a human being!
That tune—when we were kids we favored it—
    remember?

7/13/19

38 Lawes

William Lawes (1602–1645)
Consort Setts, Ayres and Dances for Viols
Fretwork: Music for Viols, CD 2 of 6
Virgin Classics

Iambic hexameter, three 2-strophe rhyme patterns
ABCD, ABCD, EFGH, EFGH, IJKL, IJKL
x/ x/ x/ x/ x/ x/

Grave overture, and greatly syncopated, leads
To quicker, yet methodical and fugal thought.
Staccato interlude is brief, and won't return:
We end the fantazy in solemn tranquil wise.

The aire is joyful, contrapuntal too. One heeds
In second fantazy, new keys to which we're brought.
The scope of colored tone an organ-breadth will learn.
Why stop? A shocking break!—a crisis—then the sighs

Of copers who the problem gratefully resolve!
Again, the ayre will copy the initial mood,
But speedy, blithe transition-movement we observe.
Prepare, in Second Sett, for meditation deep.

It is a long and fruitful journey: 'twill revolve
Ingeniously about the theme with dream endued.
The latest fantazy acquires an added verve
From running figures, brisk and vigor-quick in sweep.

The ayre is ornamented interestingly.
A dance two lower viols newly introduce:
The country coll and charming tuneful jigg will please.
When consort fantazy from quick to slow has moved,

The tempos alternate, with varied melody.
The páven string- and organ-timbres will unloose,
And changing rhythms are conveyed with ample ease
In álmain, which a suitable conclusion proved.

7/14/19

39 Verdi

Giuseppe Verdi (1813–1901)
La Traviata
Performed by Glimmerglass Opera
Cooperstown NY 7/15/19

Opening line iambic hexameter
x/ x/ x/ x/ x/ x/
iambic octameters, hexameters, pentameters,
tetrameters, dimeter, and monometer variously
patterned throughout

      La traviata, or the woman led astray,
Appeared to me to walk the perfect human path of
    righteousness:
Desiring love and pleasure in their hugest depth and
    height, no less,
        Would Violetta, singing, win the day,
      And love for him that wooed—Alfredo—she
      would vow.
    A problem, though, appeared: his father swore he'd
    not allow
The ill-advised enamored boy to marry one who'd left
    the flock.
          Parental pressure made a mock
         Of all that proves a life worthwhile—
        And now, the shock:
    Poor Violetta's conscience he attempted to beguile:
"How can Alfredo's sister—purest heart, oh sweet!—get
    married to

A worthy man who'd like to seem respectable in public
    view
                  If you
A household with your chosen one continue to
    maintain?
Renounce the wayward boy, for only so you'll truly
    gain
Redemption for his sister dear; from father,
    gratitude."
Aye, Violetta must reject her lover. Only so
    Will *sister*'s reputation whiter stay than snow!
    The Lord has made a Heaven that is well
        endued
    With *love for mere repute,* and *pleasure for the
        prude.*
Poor Violetta's been convinced that here will duty
    lie.
Regrettably, she's got consumption, and must
    quickly die.
A double punishment? Why no, a triumph in the
    sky!
All's pardoned, all forgiven, and a martyr saint is
    made.
A Swollen Superego rules the globe, and so the play is
    played.

7/15/19

40 Kodály

Zoltan Kodály (1882–1967)
Háry János—Suite
Charles Dutoit, Orchestre symphonique de Montréal
London Digital

*Iambic hexameter, three somewhat variable 2-strophe
rhyme patterns*
x/ x/ x/ x/ x/ x/

The celebrated sneeze!—but then, a graver theme:
Come wilder flying sprites who lend it vital drive...
Fast forward: we Vienna's music-clock will hear:
The fairy tale is childlike—fun is had by all.

A solitary song, in cello-voice alive,
The orchestra will lead to join in plaintive dream...
The címbalom, or hammered dulcimer, how dear—
I played those melodies! That timbre I recall!

The man who struck the keyboard sat extremely near;
He took me back to Hungary in lyric stream...
A mischievous motif of trickster! He can strive
To conquer all that comes, but—brassy, brash—a
    squall!?

Our prankster-theme returns, yet calm, bemused and
    quaint...
Oh, here is something lovely: folk-tune blithe and brisk,
And chantable in triumph—strings and horn join in,
The clarinet as well—with címbalom (my friend)!

The king arrives—and ludic tonal colors paint
The march in breezy mood—our hero fain would
    frisk...
Our life is good—more legends we will glad begin
To tell—don't sneeze at that, I ask! Our bliss won't end.

[Informal, the composer talked without constraint
At Indiana U. Though elderly, no risk
He ran, he claimed, by running—rather would he win
Good health! An IU sweatshirt we'd as gift extend.]

41 Dowland

John Dowland (1563–1626)
Lachrimae, or Seven Teares Figured in Seaven
Passionate Pavans
Five viols and lute, The Dowland Consort
Musical Heritage Society, Gramophon AB SIS

Iambic heptameter, modified Omar strophe rhyming
x/ x/ x/ x/ x/ x/ x/

The song I've known so well and, grieved, in youthful
    passion sung
Comes loved-familiar back: the dulcet, ah!, the
    honeyed tongue
New rapture lends, from one who, seër, keened my
    hapless heart.
The "Newer Tears" will vary it, woe range-expanded
    wrung.

Will "Moaning Tears" more tristful be? The mind
    admires the art
Whereby the alterations woke the hearer to impart
Attention to the giving breeze upsweeping from the
    west…
Third variant, "Sad Tears," can offer moments bright
    that dart

To view as from behind a cloud, abandoning all rest:
They strike one by surprise, but after pause the fate-
    bequest

Resume with lamentation early born in brother-soul,
Imploring destined measured calm at heavenly behest.

Of "Tears Compelled" I hear the heightened motion-
     current roll
More speedily. Of "Lover's Tears" I dream the tranquil
     goal
More nearly to approach, as chordal majors multiply...
"True Tears"—the final statement—can it heal my dule,
     my dole?

No, never hope for that... Our singing *dolens*, with a
     sigh,
Will, weeping, laud the beauty rose—the nightingale be
     nigh
With unexpected pitches piercing through, as arrowed
     lung,
The soul that sought and mourned in vain a much
     beloved eye.

7/16/19

42 Schein

Johann Hermann Schein (1586–1630)
From Ps. 150, 39, 128
Psalmen Davids sampt etlichen Motetten
und dem Te Deum
La Capella Ducale, Musica Fiata Köln, Roland Wilson
Glissando WDR 3

Iambic trimeters and hexameters
x/ x/ x/
x/ x/ x/ x/ x/ x/

Four centuries had passed
Until the manuscript of Johann Hermann Schein
Would come to light at last:
We thrill to feel the strength and intricate design.
Antiphonal, the choirs
That in cathedral hall sing praise and dire dismay:
Our terrors and desires
In widened place bring height and distance into play.

The trumpet, horn, and strings
May fortify the voices that in varied range
For Him, the King of Kings,
Will praise of every gloried instrument exchange.
In palace do we stride,
Who 'neath the roof of deepest blue and fragrant cloud
With widened heart abide,
More tall to stand, and to His will more deeply bowed.

We pray that He remove
The shame of being smitten hard by hand above;
The discipline let prove
To stalwart servant a remembrancer of love.
We rend our garment-cloth
In hope that penance, token true, received may be:
Attacked by worm and moth,
We humbly know our woe, who are but nullity.

The Selah we have sung
With every loveliness we ken that can adorn
We pray might rise among
The cloud-white angels heralding with hymn the morn.
Our children's children may
We live to see and, from the heaven, blessing hear
On Zion's triumph day,
And grateful be for grace to live the God-made year.

7/17/19

43 Mahler

Gustav Mahler (1860–1911)
Das Lied von der Erde (The Song of the Earth)
Text after Hans Bethge, Die chinesische Flöte
The Complete Symphonies and Orchestral Songs, Vol.
III, CD 3
Leonard Bernstein, Conductor
Wiener Philharmoniker, Concertgebouw Orchestra
Deutsche Grammophon

Iambic hexameter
x/ x/ x/ x/ x/ x/
Third strophe trochaic
/x /x /x /x /x /x

A song of triumph, wildness, and the sudden gust...
What are the gathered horns proclaiming, why are
     sprites
Careening through the wind? Embattled, spirit vim
Is fevered—why's the brevity of human life outraged,
By howling ape-cries mocked? The frantic, angry man
Had best drink heady wine—for dark is every breath
Which—this we can't forget—will tell of soon-come
     death.

In gardens find we rest? The jade-dust blown by wind
Prefigures chilly winter, piercing shout of pain!
The blooms of lotus, withered, float on stream—and
     heart
Aweary needs to sleep, the cares of day forget—

The devil's interval appears amid the calm,
For loneliness, that comes to all, is early known
While waters rush—with never sun in comfort shown.

    Green pavilion, porcelain, pure white the striping,
    Brightened by the lively chat of pleasant friendship,
    Prompts the country-folk to speak in gentle verses.
    Now we'll gladly watch the flower-picking maiden.
    Steeds—of what a handsome man!—tread fallen
        petals...
    Water mirrors all in soft reversal-turning:
    Autumn souls are calmed save one, the woman
        yearning.

The drunkard, drowning sorrow as he'd always done it,
Observed that overnight the spring arrived—to
    vanish...
The very birds appear to laugh—is there a teaching
To hear? We rest, we'll be refreshed—yet night
    approaches.
The moon is floating, heaven-borne, to breezes' lulling.
Yet febrile strings, exhortive horn-call agitation—
Though friend at length appears!—will countervail
    elation.

"I thank you for the drink, fine comrade wise and
    helpful—
Yet to the distant mountains I again must roam—
To find my rest, my destination, and my home."

7/17/19

44 Schütz

Heinrich Schütz (1585–1672)
Ps. 19:2–7, Geistliche Chormusik, Gesamtaufnahme
Tölzer Knabenchor, Musikalische Compagney
Gerhard Schmidt-Gaden, Conductor
Capriccio Digital

*Iambic hexameter; two rhyme patterns ABCD, then two
EFGH*
x/ x/ x/ x/ x/ x/

The boy and trumpet tell God's Maker-plenitude.
The chorus quick repeat the earth-and-heaven
    thought.
The tenor and the youth describe the colloquy
Wherewith the creatures of the universe concur.

The chanters and the brass and choir have been
    endued
With quick conviction, to the selfsame purpose
    brought.
Tones low and high are joyed by sun arising: he,
A bridegroom-hero, shining will the world bestir.

The music follows when the text will rhythm shift.
The strings and brasses, the adult and youth combine
Their varied paths in clever counterpoint as do
The cosmic elements that love-impelled converse.

Reply and intertwining may the spirit lift.
A grateful stimulus to me—the grand design:
The doxological reply resounding through
The mind will hearts of all in concord wide immerse.

7/18/19

45 Villa-Lobos

Heitor Villa-Lobos (1887–1959)
Preludes No. 1 in E Minor and No. 3 in A Minor
The Art of Segovia, disc 1 of 2, guitar solo
Deutsche Grammophon

Iambic hexameter
x/ x/ x/ x/ x/ x/

In tranquil Spanish hamlet, shade-tree lending breeze,
I'm writing in the meter picked for summer ease:
E Minor, graceful melody from village heart,
Schubertian, so easy-going, at the start...

The harmonies more clever grow, the tension heats—
Rubatos' brave delay impassionating beats.
If doubt be raised by ardent seeker questioning,
Resolved 'twill be when, peaceful, maiden sweet will
    sing...

In quicker threes, an up-rushed mood will overwhelm!
Do villagers reply, the two to reassure?
I think they furthered love; Theme One regains the
    helm—
The older story's told—more smiling—tender—pure.

The Prelude in A Minor pensive, brooding turns;
A thought, ascending, comes, that long scrutation
    earns.

'Twill then be reconsidered—had we something lost?
Initial scheme is back—we're baffled, wonder-tossed.

A question first awoke: was what I did worthwhile?
From every angle 'tis re-asked, in patient style.
Soliloquy, perhaps, in opera or play—
The consequences drawn will take us far away.

The auditorium would keep a silence rare
For quite a massive crowd—I'm feeling it right now.
We heard a man revered… Segovia was there!
No microphone the world-famed artist would allow.

I'd never listened harder in my youthful days.
(Can barely hear—the way that hand—half-hidden—
    plays!)
We sat enchanted, in respect and tender love…
Impalpable, the ones that hearkened from above.

7/19/19

46 Biber

Heinrich Ignaz Franz Biber (1644–1704)
Sonata XV: The Coronation of Mary as Queen of
Heaven and Earth
Rosary Sonatas for Violin and Continuo
Andrew Manze, violin and Richard Egar, organ and
harpsichord
Harmonia Mundi

Sapphic
/ x / x / xx / x / x
/ x / x / xx / x / x
/ x / x / xx / x / x
            / xx / x

Blesséd, we processional greeting offer—
Long foreknown ascent of the heav'n adoring.
All is now prepared—let the ayre be chanted,
            Graced with your favor.

Love song tender deeming it, we will vary
Tones more choicely formed with adornment added—
Then more soft, through granting of joy and comfort,
            Swathed in your mercy.

Hear the startling news of the scordatura
Pitches of the strings in the unexampled
Mode that we, inspired, are for *you* inventing—
            Rosary Tribute.

Comes a regal festival entertainment:
Souls, their thought exchanging in vivid parley,
Energy portray—the jongleur in motion,
            Leaping, cavorting.

Next—on ground, division the speed increasing,
Testing every limit of thankful gladness,
We, the heart and mind who would fain enliven,
            Hope we may please you.

Let our theme, concluding in sum-canzona,
Dolor tears recall, with a hidden piercing;
These we show with intervals oddly fallen—
            Then to the major

Coming back with equally sudden quickness!
May the sarabanda—that, lauding, follows—
Heiterkeit, serenity, calm-in-wonder,
            Give you, our Lady.

Let the variation at length appended,
Bliss convey unblemished that souls, reshapen
Wholly by delight in your sacred presence,
            Glad are imparting.

7/19/19

47 Janáček

Leoš Janáček (1854–1928)
Glagolitic Mass
Prague Radio Choir, Gewandhausorchester Leipzig,
Kurt Masur, Conductor
Philips Digital Classics

Alcaic
x/ x/ x/ xx/ x/
x/ x/ x/ xx/ x/
   x/ x/ x/ x/x
  /xx /xx /x /x

Soprano, choir, compete in despairing plea
That God and Christ have mercy, and then the strings
    Initiate the wander-motive,
    Birds and the winds and the...drums of thunder?

The tenor's cry, the choral reply combine
Their spirit-weather brooding in dark to show—
    The credo, shouted out with power,
    Fighting to stifle the ill surrounding.

The Věruju, a faith from the mountains borne
On women's breath, more tranquil refrain to grant,
    Won't countervail the horns, the organ
    Summing the chaos confronting nations.

The text the crucifying torment depicted well—
The triumph overwhelming emergent soon:

High violins a light descrying
Wait till Hosanna may fill the heavens.

The violin excitement will not let up,
For all the creatures now from the grave arise:
    The trumpets are an angel presence,
  Melody-emblems portraying, faithful.

In forest clearing, suppliants humbly ask
That sin from all the world be removed—but still
    The organ prayer, loud yet doubting,
  Mourns for the plague on the world inflicted.

When Jacob with the Angel had wrestled brave,
No vaster madding task had the struggler known!
    With drums and horns, and strings
       commanding,
  Stalwart we martyrs await redemption.

7/21/19

48 Marais

Marin Marais (1656–1728)
Sonate à la Marésienne
Viol Music for the Sun King
Spectre de la Rose
Notes by Elizabeth Liddle and Alison Crum
Naxos

Fourth asclepiadic
        /x /x x/ x/
/x /x x/ /x x/ x/
        /x /x x/ x/
/x /x x/ /x x/ x/

    Here's a work with a lively name:
What's "Maraisian" style? French, with Corelli's blent.
    Perfect union he well might claim.
Youthful memories, too, masterly has he lent.

    I Corelli and Handel played
Early on in my teens—why not Marais, as well?
    Stroke of fate!—reputations fade
When, with passage of time, viols no more impel

    Hearts to hear them—and pupils now
Won't be drawn to the tones loved at the Sun King
        Court...
    So Marais is ignored... And how
Students new to attract? I would, for one, exhort

    Teachers: hear! 'Tis a treasure rare—

This Maraisian work—valued, the skills we learn.
    Lend attention, and see what's there:
Violinists' reward? Pleasures we quickly earn.

    Pre-Handelian grandeur find
When the opening notes come to enchant the ear.
    Turn and mordent have charms combined
Which, when once we've rehearsed, learning their bliss,
        endear.

    Lightly tripping, the dancer first
Double time would present, then, with a triple boon,
    Warm Terpsichorë-bliss-immersed,
Proved the height of delight lies in a simple tune.

    Special pleasure will next ensue:
Slow and thoughtful the form, majesty-honored,
        grand—
    Yet the improvised runs endue,
Bright, with childhood élan, fondly the saraband.

    Variations requiring skill
May a cello demand—agile performer deft—
    Which can body and spirit fill,
Swift with colloquy art—bold in the swing and heft.

    Meditation a calm brings back...
Ready, friend, for the jig? Ornament, runs, and all
    We've enjoyed, who will nothing lack,
Praise a work that the world testament blest may call.

7/21/19

49 Billings

William Billings (1746–1800)
Early American Choral Music, Vol. I
His Majestie's Clerkes, Paul Hillier, Conductor
Harmonia Mundi
Notes by Richard Crawford

Ovidian dactylic hexameter distichs
/ xx / xx / xx / xx / xx / x
/ xx / xx /   / xx / xx /

Praising the Lord in the Heaven and Earth, the
        profound, the exalted,
    Changing the meters, the group—bravely creating
        a fugue,
Let Hallelujah resound over valley and forest and
        mountain—
    Any afflicted to make wholly reshapen, reborn.

If to Emmaus abandoned, despondent, oppressed you
        are walking,
    Know that a vision will come—as to apostle
        occurred.
Chanting your "Africa," make as a trumpet your
        clarion clearer:
    Joy reaches God to become solemn and gladsome
        at once.

Funeral anthem of "Samuel, Priest" will be giving us
        comfort;

Shepherd and angel in field herald celestial
    descent.
Ballad-like, natural colloquy bringing the story before
    us,
    Five-section verse will resound, strongly for
        "Shiloh" to thank.

"Jordan" of passage to blessing in laud of a choral
    outpouring
    Mirrors the bliss of the Rose, she that in Sharon
        awakes.
Truly his fruit that is sweet to the taste, under lovers'
    wide banner,
    Being of constancy shows, dove that emollient
        croons.

Brisk "Euroclydon" a rescue from tempest and peril
    depicting,
    Separate voices and crowds pray to recover their
        faith.
"Rutland" I wish I could join as entreaties require to be
    answered:
    When shall I wake in the place whither I long had
        aspired?

"David lamenting for Absalom" often I sang when much
    younger:
    "Ah, would to God I had died, turning your death
        to my own!"
Hart that is panting for waterbrooks, ev'n as my soul
    panteth after

God will a fountain attain, thirst to be quietened,
    quenched.

Gone with the multitude, I with the voice of my joy
      having entered
    Temple much longed for in times marked by
      impatient regret,
Celebrate mercy in praise, with devotion unfailingly
      grateful.
    Chant Alleluiah, my friends; Heaven itself let
      attend!

7/22/19

50 Kern and Hammerstein

Jerome Kern (1885–1945), composer
Oscar Hammerstein II (1885–1960), text
Show Boat (1927)
Performed in Cooperstown NY by Glimmerglass Opera,
7/22/19

Iambic pentameter
x/ x/ x/ x/ x/

Just turned nineteen, in nineteen sixty-two,
A five-week Russian-language learning tour
Concluding, in Helsinki, where we'd take
A test to gauge what progress we had made.
Our guide set up a splendid "Welcome Back,"
And hearing "Ol' Man River" sung for us,
With grief and happiness I nearly cried.

It stands—that monument to human fate
And freedom, daring and acceptance mild,
A tune of pain and pray'r to end it all,
A chant that finds vitality in strength,
A windbreath-gust that, Jobean and raw,
False comforters defying in their pride,
Climbs higher, deeper sinks, and thinking calms.

It sums the woe of workers at the dock
Who sweat—the new-enslaved—that whites might play.
When Julie, major actress in the show,
From insult is defended by her spouse,

And by the envy-gorged, defeated brute
Is slandered as containing "Negro blood"
So she'll be 'ignominiously' fired,

The River, seeing—nothing saying—waits.
When gambler Gaylord Nola leads away
With lover-song that proves a "make believe,"
And later, married, bankrupt, leaves—and takes
Their little daughter, who so loved them both,
A life in convent school abandonment
To lead, where she is told to "make believe,"

The River nothing said, kept rolling on.
When Julie turned to drink before at last
Regaining stardom of a showy kind;
When Nola pardoned Gaylord, met by chance,
And took him back—with sequel who can guess?—
Though pardon's at the central heart of things
And her forgiving nature all might bless—
When ups and downs, when high and lows are shown,

The River, reft of comment words might try,
Itself is down and up, is low and high.
When we're of death afraid, of life may tire,
Vitality we godlike yet desire.
Their labor's lighter who, while fate betrays,
May feel the flow that calming psalm can raise,
And prize the favor of our lengthened days.

7/23/19

51 Achron

Joseph Achron (1886–1943)
Hebräische Melodie
CD Hebräische Melodie: Die verlorene Welt des
jiddischen Schtetls
Marat Dickermann, violin, Monica Gutman, piano
Żuk Records

Amphibrachic tetrameter couplets alternating with
amphibrachic tetrameter couplets catalectic
x/x x/x x/x x/x
x/x x/x x/x x/x
x/x x/x x/x x/
x/x x/x x/x x/

My youth's coming back—and the days of my playing
The loved "Hebrew Melody," warmly portraying,
In opening tune with a niggun-like flow,
A Sabbath tranquillity, candles aglow.

A variant follows, with gathering tension—
A baffling and dizzying wild intervention
As if in the louring of cloud in the sky
A hint were conveyed that a crisis drew nigh.

A calmer piano transition, according
A path to return to what souls find rewarding,
Let distance be felt from the maelstrom: with trills
A glad expectation the melody fills...

A statement—the ending—takes leave of the gladness
And, pensive, invested with memory-sadness,
    Two phrases are heard, an impression to leave
    That, solemn and calm, might more quietly grieve.

I played it, when young, in a Heifetz edition
Of encores, and learned of the means a musician
    Might use, greater pathos to lend to the song,
    The glide of the tone of a note rendered strong

By fingerings novel, dramatic, effective...
The present performance another directive
    Employed, with contrasting concern for a pure
    Laconic simplicity, calming and sure.

Triangular thought I am now entertaining:
First Heifetz, then I, now the duo—we're gaining
    A sense of the ways that the changing of days
    May alter the sense of each musical phrase.

7/25/19

52 Bulgarian Folk Music

Song of the Crooked Dance:
Early Bulgarian Traditional Music 1927–1942
Produced by Lauren Brody
Yazoo CDs, Shanachie Entertainment Corp.

Ovidian dactylic hexameter distichs
/ xx / xx / xx / xx / xx / x
/ xx / xx /   / xx / xx /

Dinosaur, grizzly bear, totem—no end to the rapt
        fascination
    We in "Museum" would feel, "Natural History"
        named...
Ah, but on Saturday! That's when the ethnic
        performers elation
    Granted to Sarah and me. Ardor and vigor
        enflamed

All the Bulgarian players on brass and on bagpipe. My
        fingers—
    Seven or five of them—look!—raised in a
        questioning way:
Had I an accurate grasp of the rhythms? Fine memory
        lingers:
    Nod from the leader affirmed: I'd been attentive
        that day!

Here are the sevens again—at the wedding we're
        dancing, rejoicing:

Bagpipe untiring provides oddest of meter once
more...
Dimo's announcing to Rada some tidings; and, brash,
will be voicing
Bold clarinet a reply—feelings they freely outpour.

Bear-handler singer in simple six-eight and a fiddler
together
Yield to the gaida, the pipes. Meter is rather
unclear...
Listenings many and careful may likely reveal to me
whether,
Casting old habit aside, training is aiding my ear.

Now we've a singable waltz with accordion-helped
violinning,
Then comes another in form freer with ornaments
fine.
Both are by women performed, vocal timbres from
listener winning
Thanks for their richness and depth, loved as the
countryside-wine.

Here is a vivid achievement—elopers have made their
decision:
Matchmakers calculate. Why? Status parental to
guard!
Rebels made brave are convinced they'll encounter but
little derision:
Living with elders and rules—*that* in our youth-
time is hard!

53 Haydn

Joseph Haydn (1732–1809)
Six Late Piano Sonatas
The Glenn Gould Collection Vol. 13
SONY Classical

Fourth asclepiadic
  / x / xx / x /
/ x / xx / / xx / x /
  / x / xx / x /
/ x / xx / / xx / x /

Sonata in D Major Hob. XVI:42

Treasured tone in the still surround:
Every voice will portray character purely phrased—
 Variation precision-crazed:
Nano-second the touch, lending the soul more sound.

 High the tension, and yet the mood
Cradled softly in place, held by the quiet air,
 All but love for the tune eschewed:
Ending's quite an Amen—tender the guidance rare.

 Four-note groups have a shape that's made
Once and only for each—feeling, complete, unique:
 Lover-focus the stroke will seek
Which we never regret—holy the moment prayed.

Sonata in C Major Hob. XVI:48

Quiet deepened, suspense attuned:
Fountained out of the soul, gentleness unexcelled.
    Hurried worldly distraction quelled,
Nerves on heaven-alert, love is the unimpugned.

    Contemplation with sovran pow'r,
Alteration in thought meeting with calm surprise,
    Made the lowest of tones a flow'r
Which—mute night on the earth—startled the spirit-
        eyes.

    Every second you spend today
Widened value acquires, mindfully gazed upon;
    New identity calls, to dawn
When with heart come alive, testament-art you play.

7/27/19

54 Mozart

Wolfgang Amadeus Mozart (1756–1791)
Mozart-Horowitz
Vladimir Horowitz, piano
Deutsche Grammophon Masters

Ovidian dactylic distichs
/ xx / xx / xx / xx / xx / x
/ xx / xx /   / xx / xx /

Piano sonata in B flat major, K. 281 (189f)

Pure, preternatural, delicate, deity-given precision
    All in a lyrical sweep, driven by inner desire,
Means we'll be glad the performer would kindly and
        wisely envision
    Each of the parts to repeat, done as the forces
        require.

Slow, amoroso, with love we are thinking—half
        walking, half dancing,
    Wondering how what we plan might have been
        meant to turn out...
Problems like these we've considered before, but today
        we're enhancing
    Pleasure of thought more relaxed, happily glancing
        about.

None but a god does a rondo with heaven-cavorting so
        agile:

Higher the realm of the mind opened to viewing
     today.
Mercury's quicksilver light is bewingéd and flexible.
     Fragile?
Never!—caducëal flight apt in hermetical play.

Piano sonata in C major, K. 330 (330h)

Here I'll begin in the middle, the canorous thought,
     moderato:
     Seems we are told to compose lyrical syllables deft.
Major to minor and back—we'll intone them with
     mildest vibrato,
     Calmly consistent throughout, never let down or
     bereft.

Much of the happiness had, from the quick allegretto I
     picture
     Sung on theatrical stage, comes from the joy of the
     sport:
No one can equal the athlete who never knew limiting
     stricture—
     Pindar the racer had praised: he the gods' favor
     might court.

Adagio in B minor, K. 540

Often the monologue pauses, and, too, on a chord
     unexpected:
     Doubt in chromatics might wake, yet will resolve
     be attained.

Thinking it over, the coda will ponder the matter,
      directed
    Soon on an improvised path, after an aim...that is
      gained.

7/27/19

55 Turkish Folk Music

Ashiklar, Those Who Are in Love:
Folk Music of Turkey
Ashik Masouni Serif and Other Artists, vocals and saz
Golden Horn Records

Iambic hexameter; rhyme pattern ABCDEF throughout
x/ x/ x/ x/ x/ x/

A syncopated song in minor mode, relaxed.
More active second lyric, storytelling feel.
The third in couplet lines with count of ten for each.
The áshik, who's in love, the saz may demonstrate,
A lute of medieval type: he'll improvise.

A simple tune of questioning: not overtaxed,
The lutanist will show an agile craft, ideal.
Twinned instrumental tunes a raga mood will teach:
The scale, when chosen, had been fixed—we then await
What paintings of diverse impression might arise.

A folksong my attention, bafflingly, had maxed:
Might alternating beat-schemes thematize the spiel?
The Pir, a Sufi elder, hopes that he may reach
A true devotion with a chant that shall elate.
Ambitious, he, in will to soar to higher skies.

I'm minded of the way, with tones that waned or waxed
Not greatly in their volume, on an even keel

The zikr, list of Names of God, in holy speech
Of Sufi rite I heard. The heart in high estate
To every word replies, our deep Divine surmise.

7/29/19

56 Ockeghem

Johannes Ockeghem (ca. 1410–1497)
Alma Redemptoris Mater, from Cathedral Sounds
René Clemencic, Clemencic Consort
SONY BMG Arte Nova Classics

Iambic octameter; rhyme scheme ABCDEF
x/ x/ x/ x/ x/ x/ x/ x/

The counter-tenor boy, the tenor grownup, early-time
    trombone
Conduct the praise of Mary. Youthful tones begin; each
    longer line
The man will chant, until the Lady's calm laudation be
    proclaimed.
The trio offer counterpoint in forthright independent ways
That fit together as the parts of this cathedral where
    we stand.

I offer thanks today for what by heaven-will is made my
    own.
I'm carried to the castle of the Lord through wise
    reward-design
To set before me what might be desired for one that
    newly Named
Would visit pay to time and place where laud of Light
    he'd fitly raise:
The pilgrim gift is granted, that the wilderness be
    promised land.

7/31/19

57 British Folk Music

Nowell Sing We Clear (group name and CD title)
John Roberts, Tony Barrand, Fred Breunig, Andy Davis
Voices, concertina, accordion
Golden Hind Music

Iambic tetrameter and trimeter
x/ x/ x/ x/
*   x/ x/ x/*

When angels watched their flocks by night
*   All seated on the ground*
*   —Old Foster*

A strange and hesitating mood
   Had pestered me for days.
What held me back? With bliss endued
   I fain would render praise,
   I fain would render praise,
   I fain would render praise.

I feared I'd gravely weakened be—
   Prevented, then, to write,
Nor fitting tribute melody
   Bring forth to heaven flight.
   Bring forth to heaven flight.
   Bring forth to heaven flight.

Two days I waited, till at last
   A psalm upon the third

Came down to break the hymning fast
    And on the earth be heard,
    And on the earth be heard,
    And on the earth be heard.

Roars thunder while I strike the keys
    Emboldening my soul.
It proud expands my heart with ease,
    That force may onward roll,
    That force may onward roll,
    That force may onward roll.

7/3/19

58 Beethoven

Ludwig van Beethoven (1770–1227)
Twelve Variations on a Theme from Handel's Oratorio,
Judas Maccabaeus
Richard Locker, cello; Martha Locker, piano
CD Jewish Cello Masterpieces II
Leggiero Records

Dactylic hexameter with double catalexis
/xx /xx /xx /xx /xx /

Simple and plain is the theme, and a solo for keyboard
    ensues.
Modest the both of them, surely, and pleasant the
    prospect one views.
Triplet accompaniment the advancing piano will seize,
Cello with pace never harried but tranquil and happy,
    at ease.

Speedier foursomes are dashing ahead, and the
    chording is brave.
Then comes a quiet lament on the cello, Hebraic and
    grave.
Quiet the colloquy now: they reply to each other,
    relaxed.
Cello in triplets awaking more brisk than our spring-
    breath, re-maxed.

What are the eighths in their race temerarious wishing
    to do?

Seems a debate has blown open a secret that someone
  may rue...
Hear ye!—the conquering hero at last will the cello
  make known
Grand in the strength of demand that a king be
  deposed from a throne.

Pleasant Schubertian melody, pensive and loving and
  kind...
Keyboard is prominent first, then the cello, caressing,
  how sweet!
Finally, jocular waltzing the tensions throughout will
  unwind.
Judas!—the armor is gone!—and the lady-love swept
  off her feet!

8/3/19

59 Liszt

Franz Liszt (1811–1886)
Années de pèlerinage: Deuxième année—'Italie':
VII. Après une lecture de Dante (Fantasia quasi Sonata)
CD Brahms, Liszt & Schumann: Works for Piano
Mark Anderson, piano
Notes by Michael Pipe
Nimbus Records

Iambic octameter
x/ x/ x/ x/ x/ x/ x/ x/

Diabolus in musica—the devil interval—in this—
Announcement? proclamation?—then the wonderings
    and mutterings...
We barely guess.. Intensity is undirected. Dreadful
    things
Are feared and thought of, avalanches conjured down,
    to hit or miss...

And yet a hint of bold resolve's awaking here—and
    there—before
'Twill die in silence. From a higher register faint wings
    appear...
A lover-serenade? Aubade? What time of day or eve? I
    hear
From upper sky and lower, troubled pondering, a
    mental war...

We've reached the middle point, I think, and now it's
    happened: love is free

To state an affirmation! Wait—disquiet, doubt—can
    hope avail?
It may, it must, it will, we more-than-pray, to blazing
    heav'n we sail:
Oh, buffeted by stormy force we kenned—of course!—
    that we would be!

An unawaited break, a long one... Raindrops of a dewy
    dawn—
Soft light—but followed by a castigating, pounding
    onslaught on
The ones whom shards of ice would part—with stormy
    four-direction blast
A full-stop on the judgment placed—our lovers,
    fainting, fail at last.

8/4/19

60 Brahms

Johannes Brahms (1833–1897)
Variations on a Theme by Robert Schumann, E flat
major, Op. 23
Claire Desert, Emmanuel Strosser, two pianos
Virgin Classics

Iambic heptameter
x/ x/ x/ x/ x/ x/ x/

To hymn-like loving song a variation gladly will
A treble obbligato add, ingenious and serene.
A one-and-two-and meter will in vigor supervene.
Then next, a dotted-rhythm-wind that lover-sail can
    fill.

A slower thought in minor, sober tones of bronzen
    bells.
We're swaying now in barcarolle, our gondola in
    waves—
A triplet maelstrom, frenziedly and near-insanely
    raves—
But tender doublet ripple-rhythm kinder tiding tells.

The water's getting choppier—we're quite at sea today!
A dance 'twill be for Halloween—grotesque, robust, and
    fierce—
We're safely back on land, by now, and yet the
    lightnings pierce!
Aha, we're slowing down—we march—and solemnly I
    pray.

In chorus we are singing very gently while we tread—
The primal theme is coming back. The clanging bells
    ahead
Are getting louder... Final triumph blending with a
    calm
Re-forms the heaven-melody to mourner-blessing balm.

8/4/19

61 Barber

Samuel Barber (1910–1981)
Music for a Scene from Shelley, Op. 7
Item 4 on CD Adagio for Strings &c.
David Zinman, Baltimore Symphony Orchestra
Notes by Anthony Burton
Decca

Hear'st thou not sounds in th' air which speak the love
Of all articulate beings, feelest not
Th' inanimate winds enamored of thee? List!
　　　　　—Shelley, Prometheus Unbound II.5.35–37

First two strophes amphibrachic pentameter with
catalexis, third strophe dactylic pentameter with double
catalexis
x/x x/x x/x x/x x/
/xx /xx /xx /xx /

The quarter and double-eighth melody trying to rise
We barely can hear in the timbre of string or of brass.
Collisions inconsonant... Countering bronzen descent,
A passage will climb, gaining power—our breathing is
　　hard!

The currents are joining! A hymning of hope we
　　surmise
Will come with the calm: violins that will sing can
　　surpass
In melody strength, triple-time, what we've known—
　　and we're meant

By trumpet and drum to be still, contemplation
    unmarred...

    Wavelike the glide of the strings... In the air one
        descries
    Wingéd vibrations aflutter: Dark water will glass
    What on the current may move, let from heaven be
        lent,
    After the struggle, a night-time more happily
        starred.

8/4/19

62 Stravinsky

Igor Stravinsky (1882–1971)
Concerto for Piano and Wind Instruments
(Revised version, 1950)
Philippe Entremont, piano
CD 10, Works of Igor Stravinsky on 22 CDs
SONY BMG

Trochaic octameter catalectic
/x /x /x /x /x /x /x /

Stately dotted-rhythm, slow and grand, baroque the
    overture.
Madcap theme, obrumpent, festive, plays the fitting
    role, for sure.
Woodwind groups will have their say when, undeterred
    and bursting in,
Force of stormy verve will serve piano-master... *He*
    must win.
Wouldn't overstate it, though—the world is made of
    energy:
Each can change at will to suit the others' mood, for
    youth is free!

Largo plods along till trumpets introduce a troubled
    call:
Winds reply more gently—horns keep blaring—oddly,
    after all
Declarations interrupted, keyboard starts a reverie:
None can tell where this will lead. We watch and wait
    attentively...

Deeper meditation comes, which isn't moving very
    fast…
Temper fit—frustration!—calm of comfort settling in at
    last?

Many-measured sequences the keyboard, plentiful,
    provides—
'Twixt a march and dance a shape awakens, though
    the pattern hides—
Dialogues are loud—they shout! Piano called a
    startling halt—
Might the solemn heart of starting overture new calm
    exalt?
No!—the mischief maker, unrelenting, who'll erupt
    once more,
Joking ends the colloquy with all the force we'd known
    before.

8/9/19

63 Lully

Jean-Baptiste Lully (1632–1687)
Première Suite: Le Bourgeois Gentilhomme, 1670
CD L'Orchestre du Roi Soleil: Symphonies,
Ouvertures, & Airs
Le Concert des Nations, conductor Jordi Savall
AliaVox

Iambic hexameter
x/ x/ x/ x/ x/ x/

Each double-dotted note of slow-beginning tone
To me is felt as wholly sprightly from the start.
A three-four dance more festal feeling will impart.
A string-and-wind gavotte—court's gladness amply
　　shown!

A visible dimension to the aural art—
Preserved, emergent from my child-impression grown
To fuller blossoming—a joy undimmed makes known
With comedy-ballet that once aroused my heart

In pageant-film of France! Each costume, color-burst
Upon the screen!—the bourgeois "gentleman" receives
The kind of princely treatment he, naïf, believes
To be his right—in regal culture he'd immersed

Ambition and imagining. No "truth" bereaves
The avid pupil who from middle class the first
Has been of all his line the role to have rehearsed
Of new-schooled nobleman: to Grand Ideal he cleaves.

Now lovely Daughter plans a tricky masquerade,
Her Boyfriend bringing forth in silk and jewels clad—
The "scion of the Turkish sultan"! Happy lad—
To richest entertainment glad to lend his aid!

A dance, in the Canaries claimed to have its birth,
By ceremony-entrance tune will followed be:
The violin a Spaniard-Gypsy melody
Will offer, flute-drum jig with verve occasion mirth.

The Clowns and Harlequins procession will present,
Majestic, if by metric oddities beset.
Their soothing-soft chaconne the listener will let
In comfort rest, the adolescents' kind intent.

8/10/19

64 Weinberger

Jaromír Weinberger (1896–1967)
"Polka and Fugue"
Schwanda der Dudelsackpfeiffer (1926)
Recording recalled from grade school in the '50s

Ovidian dactylic hexameter distichs
/ xx / xx / xx / xx / xx / x
/ xx / xx /   / xx / xx /

Wondering what I could write, I encountered a bright
    recollection:
    Schwanda! His polka and fugue! Vital, alive, they
        awoke!
What was the teacher intending to show us, her restive
    young pupils?
    Counterpoint play is a game—punch-lined,
        melodious joke.

One of the longest of themes that a fugue ever had, I
    imagine,
    Offered a sketch of a boy. He on the bagpipe would
        play—
This, in an opera found (the composer was Czech—but
    the title
    Given in German I still clearly recall from that
        day).

Point of a fugue is to follow the theme and enjoy where
    it leads you:

Watch while it scampers about, haply discovering
how
Mirrors of you and your wishes and drives will appear
in the people
Meeting you—yes, we're alike! Life is more curious
now.

Where is the joke I was talking about? I will gladly
explain it.
Just when you think that the fugue total fulfilment
had reached,
Comes in a moment of sudden surprise, reawakened,
the polka!
How is it possible? *Lord* knows!—every limit is
breached!

8/12/19

65 Boyce

William Boyce (1711–1779)
Symphonies
Ross Pople, London Festival Orchestra
SONY BMG

Dactylic hexameter
/xx /xx /xx /xx /xx /x

Symphony movement? or merely a song or a dance
  tune to sing with?
Suite in three parts—we've a quick and enlivening
  musical tonic—
Each an infusion of briskness and vigor, a freshening
  fling with
Rapid experiment-testing—the *song* will precede the
  symphonic.

Back to my teenager mood-life—impulsive, impatiently
  zestful—
Even while pensive, reluctant to hinder the sweep of
  the meter:
Clear affirmation confirming we're healthy and
  strong—'tis a restful,
Calming return to a youth when a moment felt longer
  and sweeter...

Fast menuetto—a little surprising—they're commonly
  slower...
All the allegros, Handelian, grandly and amply are
  cheering.

Pleasure of boat-ride—propelled by the rhythm, reliable
    rower:
Even vivace's non troppo—gavotte is unforced and
    endearing.

Symphony 6—a baroque, sober overture, then with a
    vernal
Game where the squirrels, a trio, are scampering,
    chasing, and leaping:
Tender larghetto: Pray listen to love I would fain make
    eternal!
Lulling both you and myself I'm in heaven while
    dreaming unsleeping.

Triple the rhythm the procreant fugue in the seventh
    assuming,
Glad violins are in bliss—every motion their joy is
    advancing!
Haydn himself would be hearkener-heart never better
    illuming:
Fugal and bugle at once come the huntsmen, our idyll
    enhancing!

8/16/19

66 Bruch

Max Bruch (1838–1920)
Schottische Fantasie Op. 46
Itzhak Perlman, Israel Philharmonic Orchestra,
Zubin Mehta
Notes by Christopher Field
EMI Records, Ltd.

Iambic hexameters and iambic tetrameters
x/ x/ x/ x/ x/ x/
x/ x/ x/ x/ x/ x/
    x/ x/ x/ x/
    x/ x/ x/ x/

The dreamer—let him think of all the singers gone:
Whenever one returns, the past comes back alive.
    Ahead we stride, inspired to strive
    As did each pilgrim long passed on.

Here comes the one who sang enrapt in castle while
The hearer touched with noble simple grandeur cried.
    I'd gladly join you! When I've died
    I fain would yet ensoul your style.

Rhapsodic triple time—the flute and violin
Will rhapsodize together till the men march forth.
    Fresh petrichor in dewy north—
    Most tender singing will begin:

"I'm down for lack of Johnnie"—Sad, but glory be!
Depression cannot last—Awake with "Scots wha hae"!
        Let riant variations play
        Till triumph has delivered me!

May "Auld Rob Morris" wake the violin and lyre
To show that ardent love, the source of all our breath,
        More strong than war must conquer death,
        Must draw the heart forever higher.

8/16/19

67 Burns

Robert Burns (1759–1796)
The Gardener Wi' His Paidle
Robert Burns: The Complete Songs, Vol. I, Song 1
Sung by Tony Cuffe
Linn Records

Iambic tetrameters and trimeter
x/ x/ x/ x/
x/ x/ x/ x/
x/ x/ x/ x/
*   x/ x/ x/x*

I wish I'd been brought up to sing
What here has made my love take wing
Who Scotland picture in the spring—
    The gärdner wi' his paidle.

The crystal water, merry bird
Around him when the Scotsman heard
He'd been to composition spurred—
    The gärdner wi' his paidle.

Who's early risen with the hare
May feel the bliss of heaven there
With morningtide abiding fair—
    The gärdner wi' his paidle.

When dusk will hasten to the earth
His work he leaves, that man of worth,

To share with loved one evening mirth—
  The gärdner wi' his paidle.

Blest Robert Burns, who are to me
An angel guest, your melody
I wish far better kenned might be—
  The gärdner wi' his paidle.

For Scottish people you have made
Sweet gifts upon the table laid
That savored are by man and maid—
  The gärdner wi' his paidle.

You've quite inebriated me,
The reader of my hymn will see:
Praise pride of inebriety!—
  The gärdner wi' his paidle.

8/16/19

68 Scriabin

Alexander Scriabin (1872–1915)
Five Preludes, Op. 74 (1914)
Allison Brewster Franzetti, piano
Michael Redmond, notes
ScriabinRaveldeFalla Amapola Records

Anapestic tetrameter
xx/ xx/ xx/ xx/

Douloureux, déchirant

She is trying to let semi-question come through:
'Tis repeated in vain—one the thought might
    rephrase—
Hateful-terrible topic she'd rather not raise:
Yet she can't move away—it keeps blocking the view.

Très lent, contemplatif

"Slow, contémplative"—yes but the faltering pace...
Tones chromatic in brooding will change not at all
The perspective, oh bothersome!—heart to appall...
Moving ever more slowly—bad fate, how to face?

Allegro drammatico

Theme "Perplexity" comes, and will grow more intense:
Flanked by quarter-notes, tumbling sixteenths leading
    down—

Things get louder, not better—one, shut-mouthed, will
    frown
Then explode in frustration—the mounting offense!...

Lent, vague, indécis

Quiet. Triple-beat time—we've a hint of a dance—
In ascending progression the tones of a hope.
But the theme, coming back, will be halted. We grope
For moment, then stop. We've no plan to advance.

Fier, belliqueux

We are gathering force—but direction there's none.
She is driven to yell at the blockage of thought!
What a state of exhaustion the nerve-wrath has
    wrought!—
Louder shouts!—then collapse... We are done for. We're
    done.

8/18/19

69 Ravel

Maurice Ravel (1875–1937)
Valses nobles et sentimentales (1911), first four of eight
Allison Brewster Franzetti, piano
Michael Redmond, notes
ScriabinRaveldeFalla Amapola Records

Trochaic octameter catalectic
/x /x /x /x /x /x /x /

Modéré—très franc

Noble? Sentimental? Michael Redmond called them
    "sweet" and "sour."
Double may we find the source of lively yet "ironic"
    pow'r.
Moderate and frank, melodic-dissonant, a mixed
    appeal—
Final bars—a charming, sudden harmony—surprise!—
    ideal!

Assez lent—avec une expression intense

Steady, measured pace, reflective, heavier with hint of
    doubt;
Following the train of thought, a calmer mood is
    coming out:
Graceful note-adornments caught my pleased attention
    at the first;
Odd, unstable, wander-chords throughout—I'm still in
    doubt immersed.

Modéré

Tripping-quick, with clever hemiolas, loved in happy
     days,
Interrupted now at times, the mode reshaped in
     grownup ways...
Back-and-forth go past and present, blended, then
     apart once more:
Memories returned are welcome—soon, though, fade
     the days of yore.

Assez animé

Two the triple measures which with doubled threes are
     switched and keep
Alternation unrelenting—might the hearer fall sleep
Realizing: ironizing never spies an end in sight?
Movement is its own excitement—melancholy travels
     light.

8/18/19

70 de Falla

Manuel de Falla (1876–1946)
Concerto for Harpsichord or Piano (1926)
Allison Brewster Franzetti, piano
Bronx Arts Ensemble
ScriabinRaveldeFalla Amapola Records

First 8 lines iambic hexameter
x/ x/ x/ x/ x/ x/
Next 8 lines trochaic hexameter catalectic
/x /x /x /x /x /

I'm minded of the Three Musicians painting, where
I'd view it in my teenage years. Creation flair
Had meant the pattern maker never sought but found
In seeming random patches more than thought might
    dare.

So here with brash intrusion, rhythms are unbound,
That herald, each, another theme: let *that* resound
Awhile till next an interruption sudden rise,
And unifying street-musician theme at last be crowned.

    Second movement: solemn crying psalming hies
    Upward, jubilant and energetic, vies
    Even with the wild reminders of our woe,
    Trouble vast to conquer. Stream with rain, ye skies!

    Villagers will dance to laud the stormy flow!

Jester, motley-costumed, drunken-crazed may
   show
Life our Source of Being praise in freshened air:
More than mad or sane, this hymn to A and O!

8/19/19

71 Fanny Mendelssohn and Eichendorff

Fanny Mendelssohn (1805–1847)
Frühling (Joseph von Eichendorff)
Fanny Mendelssohn Lieder
Lan Rao, soprano, Micaela Gelius, piano
SONY BMG

Trochaic tetrameters, alternating regular and catalectic
/x /x /x /x
/x /x /x /

Swirling, swooping, swift ascending,
    Breezes birth to hymn will give.
Triplets, jig-like meter lending,
    Fire the mind and cry, we live!

Fragrance brought by spring the flying
    Pinion exultation grants—
Love bemused with smiles and crying
    Rapt in plenilunar dance!

Moon and stars a voice are finding
    In the wind-excited trees
That rejoice in prophesying
    What the singing spirit frees!

She is mine! will rise and hover
    While the nightingale alone
Will bespeak the fevered lover
    Into Pre-Creation thrown!

8/20/19

72 Wolf and Mörike

Hugo Wolf (1860–1903)
An eine Äolsharfe
Mörike Lieder
Mitsuko Shirai, mezzo soprano, Hartmut Höll, piano
Capriccio Digital

Ovidian dactylic hexameter distichs
/xx /xx /xx /xx /xx /x
/xx /xx /   /xx /xx /

Softlier stroking the wind-harp, the breeze my entreaty
    had welcomed:
    Bearing your fragrance, come near, friend, from
        the burial-mound!
Longing is growing, and seizing my being—a pause in
    the wind-breath
    Only will lend it more strength, filling my senses,
        my heart...

Muse of the air, of aroma, of memory, here to my
    terrace,
    Kindly melodious come, summon with rose-breath
        to mind
Fresh-greening hillock, the one where—O sorrow!—my
    loved one is buried!
    I'd have collapsed had you not, silent, allowed me
        to sigh...

Raucously, roused!—what a wildness you wake when
    you cry on the harp-string!
  Scattering petals—they fall—even as we and our
    woe.
Souls yet unborn, you will hear how the spirit-wind
    comforts the hearer—
  Tone, you aspire and are calmed, lending my spirit
    a pray'r.

8/20/19

73 Borodin

Alexander Borodin (1833–1857)
Quintet in C Minor for Two Violins, Viola,
Cello, and Piano
Ottó Kertész, cello, Ilona Prunyi, piano,
New Budapest Quartet
Borodin Chamber Music
Marco Polo

Iambic hexameter
x/ x/ x/ x/ x/ x/

A Russian conversation, people trading 'round
An olden theme that says Beloved Past Refound.
Each eager speaker wants to play the tune right
    through
Till others join the quick "divisions on a ground."

A fugal scherzo'd festive day has not a few
Delights, the balalaika aiding: rendezvous
Of cousins with their eager children: ludic spree—
Until a mood-change overcomes the company:

A pastoral nostalgia, rustic reverie
With certain soft re-dreamings of the jubilee
One felt already at the start—and now—a leap!
A dance! a blithe kazátske!—Mama, look at me!

A toast! The kids are racing 'round the room. They
    keep

The grownups busy—brief the break—and then—the
    sweep—
The sweets of memory—loud chorus let resound!
We love you, Mother Russia, with a love most deep!

8/20/19

74 Reger

Max Reger (1873–1916)
Sonata in D Major, Op. 91, No. 2
from Three Sonatas for Unaccompanied Violin
Ulrike-Anima Mathé
Dorian Recordings

Sapphic
/ x / x / xx / x / x
/ x / x / xx / x / x
/ x / x / xx / x / x
     / xx / x

Comes dear Love ashine with a springtime intro!
New and older themes we alike shall welcome—
Sun and breeze and blue—on a tropic seashore
    Strolling, we're joyful.

Pensive, rested, turn we awhile to brooding:
Calm and tension weighed in a sweet larghetto...
Songs alone, then vocals for two in concord—
    Solo, and sharing.

Hop-skip vivacissimo, triplets fleeting;
Noble, then, with measured, serene demeanor,
Slower time, for pondering best engendered—
    Varied, our mood-frame.

Taking eighteenth-century dancing meter,
Adding modern skill of extreme precision—
Answer made to Bach with the double-stopping—
        Love is triumphant.

8/20/19

75 Moussorgsky

Modest Moussorgsky (1831–1889)
Song of the Flea (sung by Mephistopheles
in Goethe's Faust)
Feodor Chaliapin, Bass-Baritone
A Portrait: The Great Recordings (1907–1928)
Minerva

Iambic heptameter couplets with catalexis in mid-first line
x/ x/ x/x   x/ x/ x/
x/ x/ x/ x/ x/ x/ x/

Who better than Chaliapin, of noble Flea to tell?
The favorite at royal court, It cast a regal spell.

"The king a velvet frock-coat the tailor made to sew,
That Flea the fitting dignity of latest mode might show.

The Queen and all her Fraeuleins—they barely might
    survive:
So bitterly they're bitten they can scarce remain alive.

The Flea became prime minister, with ribbon and with
    star,
And hordes of fleas would follow It; they know where
    nobles are.

And no one tried to swat It—no touch would Flea
    permit.

With *us* 'twould quickly smothered be, and that's the
    end of it."

Mephisto wrote this ditty—with gloating and with glee.
Pray God preserve us humble folk whose leader is a
    flea.

8/21/19

76 Martinů

Bohuslav Martinů (1890–1959)
Duo Concertant for Two Violins and Orchestra (1937)
Works for Violins and Orchestra
Jan Pospichal and Florian Zwiauer, violins
Vienna Symphony, Marcello Viotti
Arte Nova Classics

Iambic hexameter
x/ x/ x/ x/ x/ x/

1 Poco allegro

Motivic rhythm as the major force and drive
With metrical propulsion tutti-theme begins
Alive and winning and persistent, yet in play
Are little lyric duos from the violins.

The two are concertino, coupled, it appears,
In tight-combined melodic and inventive strains:
At times the bigger group, orchestral, emulates
The lyric trend as well, and balance firm attains.

The dissonant and unabating power shows
A big Stravinsky input. Songful interludes,
However, charm the ear so greatly, and cohere
With such delight that all's resolved—no thought of
    feuds.

2 Adagio

The violins agree in depth and dolor both:
They help each other to survive the test of fate.

A hymn has grown, quite self-composed, of blended
   thought,
And comrade-orchestra their path can follow, straight.

But as the chant a march becomes, the grievers try
Some new reflective tendencies: in strength will grow
A thrusting, struggle, striving, bafflement and doubt—
A quester-challenge, yet with comfort even so.

The harmony which at the start we heard returns:
A calming gratitude, a shining in the mind,
A tenderness outpoured—supporters, quiet, hear,
And only join in soft amen, communion kind.

3 Allegro

Percussive bursts recur, as when we'd first begun:
The anapestic and the syncopated phrase
Are each employed to make you hasten: as we run,
We energy desire, the racer to amaze.

A jaunty dance will link the shorter units now,
Until with pensive calm the orchestra prepares
A holidaying episode that will allow
More playfulness, entirely shedding grownup cares.

I feel a mood that's Brandenburgian: device
Of sequenced shouting, youthful, muscular and glad—
Paired tonal frenemies, wild outbreak to entice—
And thoroughly by all a splendid time is had!

8/27/19

77 Saint-Saëns

Camille Saint-Saëns (1835–1921)
Sonata for Violin and Piano Op. 75 No. 1 in D minor
Saint-Saëns—Debussy—Franck Sonatas
for Violin and Piano
Mirijam Contzen, violin, Valery Rogachev, piano
Arte Nova Classics

Iambic octameter, rhymed couplets
x/ x/ x/ x/ x/ x/ x/ x/

1 Allegro agitato

How perfect, how surprising, folktune-phrase! from out
the twos and threes
Arising to awake me—whom the thought of them did
not quite please...
The tune again appears!—amid a foxhunt run... You
can't foretell:
Then—back again to view the steady two-three group.
And now a spell
Is thrown by dotted rhythms that will try to bring the
mood alive.
Still, every time the folktune magic heartens, 'tis a big
High Five!

2 Adagio

Duet of threes on violin and sixes on the keyboard—
slow,

Deliberative pace, till tempo hastens, wond'ring where
    to go...
The question-answer, fiddle-and-piano shifts
    continuing
Until the two return to reinvent what they'd begun to
    sing.
They let piano take the lead, the string'd reply be
    improvised:
Their canticle in peace concludes, the partnership
    uncompromised.

3 Allegretto moderato

A butterfly on blossoms might the triplet skipping best
    portray.
The self-begotten song, that out of dance awakened,
    Spring! will say.
Duet of movements and of fresh aromas, leaping yet
    relaxed—
An intermezzo—keeps delight alive, the mind not
    overtaxed.
But here a meditation, half immersed in hymn-
    religion—why?
That super-speed Olympic race may Pindar-like exult
    the sky—

4 Allegro molto

And *that* will be the episode—no break permitted—
    which ensues!
I love it when the purer joy, mere Being, means we
    never lose

Who momently may call to mind the miracle that is our
    birth,
Discovering the fountain of our youth in endless
    heaven-mirth.
Ecstatic—we're beside ourselves and leave our ego far
    behind.
The folktune sung above comes back, and life renewed
    in this we find.

8/27/19

78 Messiaen

Olivier Messiaen (1908–1992)
Turangalîla-Symphonie (parts 1–4 on CD of 10)
Yvonne Loriot, piano, Jeanne Loriot, ondes martenot
Orchestre de l'Opéra Bastille, Myung-Whun Chung
Notes by Olivier Messiaen, tr. Paul Griffiths

Amphibrachic tetrameters, two regular, two catalectic
x/x x/x x/x x/x
x/x x/x x/x x/x
x/x x/x x/x x/
x/x x/x x/x x/

The world-film I view—geological swirling
With boulders half-molten colliding and whirling—
    Contains in part two intimations of peace—
    A Love Song? But dinosaur-tromping won't cease.

Percussion goes wild, though at intervals quiet
Is hinted—procession? Or dance? We descry it
    In righteous attempt to wave storm-winds away
    With wood block and gong that the acolytes play.

Insistence, a strength unrelenting, is imaged
In figures that staunchly conflicting are scrimmaged
    Till call to a council of wisdom be heard...
    Then—careful!—a slide and a crash undeterred.

The gamelan roams, with stentorian brasses
Confronting the random percussion in masses.

176 ♫   *Martin Bidney*

An oboe with woodblock in dialogue sounds:
Bassoon and piano are making their rounds...

The first of the Turangalîlas we've ended—
The life-and-death changefulness, blessèd, befriended...
   There's time for intensities deepened to be
   While fourths are augmented—portentous, to me.

We "ten simultaneous musics" are hearing
In Love Tune the Second... Receiving, unfearing,
   We watch ostinatos contestingly crowd—
   Piano bursts out, and our heads have we bowed...

79 Satie

Eric Satie (1866–1925)
Piano Works
John White, piano
Notes by Christine Bußmann-Kollersbeck
Arte Nova Classics

Amphibrachic hexameter catalectic, first 8 lines;
x/x x/x x/x x/x x/x x/
dactylic hexameter catalectic, second 8 lines
/xx /xx /xx /xx /xx /

"A real medieval musician"—is that what we're dealing
   with here?
Well, Claude Debussý made the claim—it intrigues
   me—so let us attend.
I'm noticing plenty of calm, repetition; assurance they
   lend,
And themes Rosicrucian loom big—so the Notes make
   abundantly clear.

He writes of the ringing of bells, and he'll vary the
   clangor with chords.
We're free to interpret the reverie: glory may well be the
   Lord's.
I'm liking the flow, the simplicity, tension and
   subsidence meek.
And here is a ground with divisions again, for the
   pilgrim to seek.

Messiaen's word: "Be aware of the ten different
  things that I say."
Never Satie. When a motive appears, we'll be
  learning it well.
Third of the Ringings the wandering-legend
  continues to tell.
Ending is quite unpredicted—things vanishing
  quickly away.

Fourth gnossienne keeps the étude-like flavor,
  adorned by the East.
Chord that concludes, unrelated, a riddle-enigma
  released.
Fifth will reshaping astray of the right-hand
  material use:
Yet may the bass-line unchanging a somnolent
  feeling effuse...

8/28/19

80 Goedicke (Гедике)

Alexander Goedicke (1877–1957)
At War (From the Diary of a Dead Soldier)
Russian Futurism, Volume II: Alexander Goedicke
Orchestral Works
Russian Philharmonic Orchestra, Konstantin Krimets
Arte Nova Classics

Iambic heptameter, modified Omar strophe rhyming
x/ x/ x/ x/ x/ x/ x/

With trumpet taps for intro, we've reluctant been to
     stir.
The horns are mustering alarm. Lament will yet
     demur.
Some halting motion, speeding up... And in the
     trenches we
May courage try to generate, whatever might occur.

Attack! Staccato, panic—but a sudden question. Or—
Is that the sound of taps returning? What is coming?
     More
Of doubtful speculation I can hear, confusingly,
With wavering attention made. A death, a closing
     door...

A silence, then the horns—a March of Mourning.
     Tremolo...
And now—the battle. Triple-timed, more triumph here
     than woe!

The ending: slow, chromatic, cello-trumpet duo. Free,
The small-talk idle, wand'ring... Then, the taps-theme.
　　Even so.

8/29/19

81 Antheil

George Antheil (1900–1959)
A Jazz Symphony for Piano and Orchestra
Michael Rische, piano
Rundfunk-Sinfonieorchester Berlin, Wayne Marshall
Piano Concertos of the 1920s:
Schulhoff, Antheil, Gershwin
Arte Nova Classics

Iambic octameter
x/ x/ x/ x/ x/ x/ x/ x/

A jazzy blasting theme of trumpets, then an absent-
    minded stroll
Of dazed piano till the crazy lightning sparkle,
    thunders roll.
A saxophone, a muted trumpet, horn and xylophone
    may throw
Some fragmentary themes about, but numbing
    rhythms onward go.

Another downpour comes from keyboard, then a
    shattered fragment-theme,
With brief piano-quiet—next returns the urge, in rebel-
    dream,
To recapitulate some dances heard in cars on radios:
An OCD impression seems, to me, not ever far from
    those.

The trumpet, horn shout back and forth while crowds
    their ostentatious fun

Pursue till energy runs out, or New York New Year's
    Eve is done.
A female vocalist in form of alto saxophone, I'd guess,
With coarsened voice from long-term smoking, chants
    in wide and fond largess.

Half drunken are the players, who their notions
    blatantly assert—
Defiance emblematic, weary worn-out habitudes to
    hurt—
But then arrives a well-known tune, with harmonies
    you'll recognize,
Piano asking, "Why be anxious? Look—I'm back!—just
    close your eyes..."

8/29/19

82 Ginastera

Alberto Ginastera (1913–1983)
Sonata for Piano (1952)
Hilde Somer, piano
Vienna Philharmonic Orchestra, Ernst Maerzendorfer
Phoenix CDs

Ovidian dactylic hexameter distichs, moving from 2
unrhymed to 2 rhymed
/ xx / xx / xx / xx / xx / x
/ xx / xx /   / xx / xx /

1 Allegro Marcato

Latin-American sounding, the meter, the soul of the
    music:
    Forceful, marcato, and low; higher and bell-like
      and soft.
Fragment of dance will be throbbing, with grace-notes
    a flowing adornment;
    Then declamation awakes: making the meter its
      theme.

2 Presto Misterioso

Night-music rapid and quiet—the scampering, darting,
    yet also—
    Memory-thanking—motif, pleasing, from movement
      the first.

Then we recur to the questioning Nature at dawn may
      awaken:
Tinier creatures will find fitting, applauding reply.

3 Adagio Molto Appassionato

Here we've a solo assurgent from tentative muted
      beginning
    (Never suppose that a key somehow might furnish
      a plan):
Passionate crisis awhile—how to tally the losing or
      winning?!—
    Pondering—long—must return; effort has done
      what it can.

4 Toccata Concertata

ONE-two-three, FOUR-five-six; ONE-and, TWO-and,
      THREE-and: *theme is a meter.*
    So will the whirlwind of tones chaos by order
      control.
Melody—yes!—will awake—for the maelstrom,
      advancing—our greeter—
    Needs to proclaim it to all: *Dancing—our life and
      our goal.*

83 Clara Schumann

Clara Schumann (1819–1896)
Waltz (lyrics by Johann Peter Lyser)
from Clara Schumann Lieder
Lan Rao, soprano, Micaela Gelius, piano
Arte Nova Classics

*Dactylic tetrameters, alternating lines with one- and
two-syllable catalexes*
/ xx / xx / xx / x
/ xx / xx / xx /

Vessels unmooring, entrancing, assuring
Never may liveliness come to an end,
Even when lyrics are gloomy, alluring
Heart that your fast-darting art will befriend,

You the Schubertian practice have mastered,
Every new stanza reshaping, reframed,
Dancing Creation, with flame Zoroastered,
Praising a maiden, Bacchantic her name!

We're to the altar by Schiller invited
Where the inebriant radiance reigns
Which our Elysium's daughter delighted:
Freely imbibing, one heaven attains.

Binding again in your kindly embracing
Cousins by custom dissevered too long,
Sister and brother with gratitude gracing,
Glad be you made by our welcoming song!

8/31/19

84 Campion

Thomas Campion (1567–1620)
Come chearfull day
The First Booke of Ayres / XVII (c. 1613)
Rachel Elliott, soprano, Mark Padmore, tenor,
Peter Harvey, baritone, Nigel North, lute
English Ayres by Thomas Campion
Linn Records

Iambic pentameter quatrain with iambic tetrameter
    couplet
x/ x/ x/ x/ x/
x/ x/ x/ x/ x/
x/ x/ x/ x/ x/
x/ x/ x/ x/ x/
    x/ x/ x/ x/
    x/ x/ x/ x/

I listen to the poem that you wrote,
With voices four melodic intermeshed:
A pair of bodies formed—each Adam-note
To soul belongs of Eve more beauty-fleshed.
    In dream, a double tutor said to me,
    "Musician, write, and lover truer be."

My dream was of a school of colloquy
Where pupils made the word each day renewed,
And where the craft of chant had speedily
Been by the gods' poetic lore endued.
    Composer, you this vision sowed
    Before I slept, and so my ode.

Symposium meant learning every day
How heart and mind in human soul were blent:
We granted were, the stations on our way
To bless when each by Name divine was lent,
    In order that we'd come to know
    How word and tone united flow.

I've written in the strophe shape you wrought
Whom I as angel of my fate would view.
For that which to my soul was lately taught
I latter years I'll yet be thanking you:
    The saints of beauty I can see
    In meter clothed, and melody.

8/31/19

85 W. F. Bach

Wilhelm Friedemann Bach (1710–1784)
Concerto per il Flauto traverso in D BR C 15
World Première Release
Die Bach-Söhne I: Wilhelm Friedemann Bach, Concerti
Karl Kaiser, flute,
Freiburger Barockorchester, Gottfried von der Goltz
Carus

Dactylic hexameter
/xx /xx /xx /xx /xx /x

Here's what I need to recall what a fest will forever be
    present!
Those with a holiday-heart and a mind for the
    frolicking-pleasant
Doubly exult when with Friedemann Bach we a score-
    resurrection
See has been gratefully made, for our sudden delighted
    inspection.
Blithe syncopation, elation, the strings are already
    foretelling;
Flute, honored guest, in good fashion is drest,
    cognoscenti enspelling.

Let us of elegant splendor partake in a tranquil and
    gracious
Dance, where the curtsying, bowing, and phrasing will
    feel efficacious.
Thus will the son at the court that is far from the
    church of his father

Favor obtain without teaching, and managing boys,
  and such bother.
Stately the attitude—grand, and a gentry-contentment
  conveying—
Happens to be what I need, psychic tension with
  kindness allaying.

Vim and vivacity welcome will prove to assisting
  musicians—
Yet, on the watch, they're alert, lest the soloist *rush*.
  Frank admissions
I have reluctantly made of the flaw when, in ensemble
  playing,
Fiddle a will of its own might assume, and from tempo
  be straying...
Skilled violinist, aware of the tendency, wary, may
  pardon
Those who with whimsical freedom are tempted to trip
  in the garden.

8/31/19

86 Wagner

Richard Wagner (1813–1883)
Mad About Wagner: The Greatest Stars,
the Greatest Music
Total Madness 72:44
Deutsche Grammophon

Dactylic hexameter
/xx /xx /xx /xx /xx /x

1 Die Walküre—The Ride of the Valkyries

Avid, adastral, thalassal, in tone-art poluphloïsboic,
Ample Imagining drawn both to sadness and triumph
   heroic,
Visit me now in a disc while I hear what was dubbed
   Total Madness:
Rouse me with power heliacal, nighttime dispelling
   with gladness!
Riding Valkyries, the stride of my living-pace willing to
   hasten,
Rising and falling, aloft reascending, delay would you
   chasten!

2 Lohengrin—Prelude, Act III

Lohengrin Prelude, you swiftly agree, and with cheer,
   in promoting
Will, that within me upraised over turmoil of worry is
   floating:

Also I'm liking the quiet relief, the emollient lyric,
Though, all too quickly (for sluggards) it yields to
    sublime panegyric
Sounds, that—implied in the skies—to the heroes of
    passion are shouting:
Be who you are, be the Present—a gift!—every lethargy
    routing.

3 Tannhäuser—Entry of the Guests

Tannhäuser, sounding the horns for to welcome the
    people expected,
Then a relaxed and a casual march that decorum
    protected,
Changing, with clarion summons, the mood to a choir-
    chant beseeming,
Fitly begotten of years that you gladly devoted to
    dreaming...
Turning from march to an anthem invoking a
    pilgriming journey,
Readiness claiming, to face all offenders in chivalrous
    tourney.

4 Tristan und Isolde—Liebestod

Tristan, Isolde, what's known as your love-death,
    instead is revealing
Passion that, lived as we feel it, is lover-dreamed
    covenant-sealing:
First, we've a wave that, caressing to soothe, turns a
    turbulent current;

192 ♩ *Martin Bidney*

Tremolos louder, while, cresting, the triplets and fours
    no deterrent
Fear or encounter: an urge that, assurgent, arising, is
    riant—
Swelling, exultant, and undulant, welling, decisive,
    defiant.

5 Tannhäuser—Pilgrims' Chorus
Andreas Schmidt, Wolfram; Cheryl Studer, Elizabeth

Solemn, the pilgrims in choir: are you, Tannhäuser,
    leaving forever?
Bond with the cave-dwelling goddess you cannot
    entirely dissever.
Ah, so the chorus with what you resolve are, united,
    agreeing?
Hear it—a hymn of assent! For they know you're
    departing, not fleeing.
Yet will the tristful good-bye be depicted in volume
    diminished:
So we accept, and more calmly—an epoch in living is
    finished.

6 Die Meistersinger von Nürnberg—Prelude, Act I

March of the Masterly Singers, my youth-flame bring
    back unabated!
I had the Overture played—and been thrilled by the
    fugue-life created—
Winding and sinuous way that the melody ever-
    evolving

Takes, with a break here and there for a gladsome but
    partial resolving.
Interludes elvish and prankish contrást with the lyrical
    ardor:
Glad violins, you rejoice in your skill, though you never
    worked harder!

7 Die Walküre—Magic Fire Music
James Morris, Wotan

Wotan is lecturing Logë—but tranquil the mood is
    becoming:
Greeting, Valkyries! The tremolos calm us, recalling
    the strumming
Spring mandolins may create; and the theme of five
    notes reinforces,
Tranquil, affirming, the flow of a stream that
    transparently courses
Over the countryside bright when the May-wind the
    field is awaking.
Here is the mood that the Idyll of Siegfried, I think,
    might be taking.

8 Twilight of the Gods—Dawn & Siegfried's
Rhine Journey

Rising of dawn from the silence. French horns offer
    calm salutation.
Rise violins to excitement. The brasses intone
    jubilation.
Rhine-journey! Siegfried a liminal place for the heart is
    traversing:

Ultimate prophesied triumph of freedom he's boldly
    rehearsing.
Trumpet-call summons—arise! and the birdcalls will
    cheer the progression!
Soon, gods will yield. Are the people prepared for the
    great supersession?

9 Twilight of the gods—Funeral March

Double the drum-call. In theme of two notes had a
    fate-stroke been stated:
That's the motif that we feel is the seed of a grief
    unabated.
Movement is nearly reduced to a waiting, a hush, and a
    stasis;
Journey to underworld visioned, katábasis being the
    basis.
Death is predicted. We hear it in softening tone that
    will vanish.
Quiet is fitting when power divine shall a tyranny
    banish.

10 Twilight of the Gods—Finale
(Immolation of the Gods)

As in the episode Love-Death, so here is the power
    ascending.
Funeral flames? And with downward cascades,
    overwhelming, unending.
Oboe announces a hope, while the strings and the
    horns lift it higher:

Something will wake from the tragic. Reborn is our
    human desire.
Twilight of gods guttered out, that were plunged into
    Stygian night,
Morning awakes—let our mourning for those be
    eclipsed by the Light.

8/31/19

87 Schnabel

Artur Schnabel (1882–1951)
Sonata for Violin Solo (1919)
Christian Tetzlaff, violin; Stefan Litwin, piano
Artur Schnabel Violin Sonatas
Arte Nova Classics

Iambic hexameter
x/ x/ x/ x/ x/ x/

1 Slow, very free and passionate

Four questions at the start. A dialogue will try
To journey toward an answer. Bar lines—they are gone.
Assertions of a varied length will multiply:
A colloquy with self the stalwart carries on.
Ah, tender, yet persistent... question-answer talk.
Faint echoes from the past... arpeggiated whim...
A soaring to the height—the brave one needn't balk:
He's been commanded, *Sing!* and 'twill suffice for him.
Diminuendo—and we end—at rest to lie.

2 With strongly-cheerful wander-pace, much life throughout

Two striking chords in starting. Reaffirming these,
Our hiker-stroller strides with freedom and with ease.
There's playful speculation, jokes and wit abound,
Some irony—strong humor covers lots of ground.
A more tradition-anchored song would glad arise,
But—whimsy yet in charge—'twill vanish in surprise.

3 Tenderly, gracefully, and always restful

The double grace-note to begin the singing phrase
A loved guitar-strum calls to mind, in small-town
      square.
We listen with attention, savoring the ayre...
Some drama's warming up—in check, though, for
      awhile:
Experimental playing, scamper-like in style,
Is trying now to focus, thinking to assert...
Long silence. Pizzicato—is the mind in tune?
We wander in harmonics, chordal plucking try.
Strange, faint, and mystic wonder-seemings in the
      sky...
We calmly take our time. We're going nowhere soon.
By pausing we become receptive and alert:
We'll pluck our loved guitar, loved mental weather fair.
No measured flight the sprites portray, but wanton
      ways...

4 Extremely fast (prestissimo)

Perpetual the motion—travel, not the goal!
The keys wherethrough we pass, the landscape
      varying,
Have matter lent for thinking. Casual, the stroll,
Despite initial plan. No, speed is not the thing.
But wait—we next return, revisit hectic flight.
A song is forming, force wherein we take delight.
The firm-coherent phrase a little game will play,
Then brightly, lightly disappear. A pleasant stay.

5. Very long half-notes, with solemn festal expression,
yet ever simple

With hints of triple time, with playful harmonies,
Duet of short and long, experimental ease,
Till pizzicato interlude will vary same.
The meters, too, are relishing an episode
Where triple tune is altered—new obsession owed
To what? A flutter-by with wingèd flight will claim
Predominance, then turn emphatic. Midpoint came—
The circling flight continues. Height it soon will reach
And in a hymn of triumph might a lesson teach:
A state of contemplation enter, and abide
To test what insight color-chording will provide.
A flutter-fadeout... Then of search another phase:
We walk in heavy threes, then stride accelerate
To find where we may well assess our wander-ways:
Last major chord—who would have thought?—desire
    will sate.

9/1/19

88 Ligeti

György Ligeti (1923–2006)
Sonata for Cello Solo
Amit Peled, cello
Cellobration (with Eliza Ching, Piano)
Notes by Sarah Adams Hoover
Centaur

Iambic hexameter; 15-line sonnet with ABCD DCBA
rhyming in octet
x/ x/ x/ x/ x/ x/

1 Dialogo—adagio, rubato, cantabile

Four deep melodic phrases—introduced, each one,
By two- or three-note pluck-percussion. Then the tune,
With integrated, fewer pizzicatos, more
Elaboration, chord-provided, broadens out.

Majestic-desperate and soul-defending shout—
As of a prisoner, a Jew, in brutal war
Confined, who hope may muster that his fate will soon
Be changed, the horrid conflict, all-too-long, be done.

2 Capriccio con slancio [rushing]

To frame a structure 'mid a people that are blind—
Wild nervous rushing, groaned augmented seconds—
    bind
The energies that throb with agitated will—

Let impulse rule!—the freedom, brief, intense—let fill
With bliss of random fashioning the harried mind,
The tension grow and swell and near explode, until

The closing chords, unstilled, unkilled, are unconfined.

9/1/19

89 Handel

George Frideric Handel (1685–1759)
from Harpsichord Suites Nos. 1–4
The Glenn Gould Edition
SONY Classical

Iambic heptameter, first two suites
x/ x/ x/ x/ x/ x/ x/
Amphibrachic tetrameter catalectic, third suite
x/x x/x x/x x/

Suite No. 1 in A major, HMV 426

A simpler tune is background in a Prelude pair with
  one
That, traveling half-improvised, a freedom-range has
  won.
The stately allemande a cordial colloquy maintains,
Then muted-plucked with pedal an exotic timbre gains.
Courante is catchy, singable, and, glad, remains with
  me:
The gigue, I love the most—imprisoned spirit will it
  free!

Suite No. 2 in F major, HMV 427

Adagio [attacca] will the plucked effect resume:
The ornaments arouse while the melodic strains
  illume.
With superhuman speed the brave Allegro rushes by,

Each tone a word of life to such an auditor as I.
Once more a declamation, operatic-style, is heard—
Let hearer by the fugue, in fit concluding tune, be
    stirred!

Suite No. 3 in D minor, HMV 428

The warm-up is rapid. In fugue that succeeds
Will hero recount his imperious deeds.
Let sweet allemande by a suitor be sung
In—ever delightful—an amorous tongue!
(The meter I seem to be switching—and why?
'Twould seem I'm entranced by the smile and the sigh.)
Courante is a little bit slower than most,
Though, too, 'twould for words be an excellent host.
An air is arriving: remember it well:
In multiple forms 'twill abide for a spell.

In variant one it is placid and calm,
For mental disturbance a merciful balm,
While variant two "a division" we name:
With double the notes, it may kinship yet claim.
In variant three there's a triplet-ing move;
The fourth variation most dazzling will prove!
The presto—impressive! Conclusion will, too,
A rhythm for dancing be granting to you.

9/1/19

90 Rorem

Ned Rorem (1923–)
Eleven Studies for Eleven Players (1959)
Ned Rorem: The Louisville Orchestras
Jorge Mester, Robert Whitney, conductors
Jerome Lowenthal, piano
First Edition Music

Amphibrachic hexameter catalectic
x/x x/x x/x x/x x/x x/

To many percussing at once comes the trumpet
    displaying the thcmc.
The friends' allegretto with instruments (nine of them)
    blend in a stream.
A bird call brings vague intimations while, muffled, the
    company doze.
A diary-page violin will her memories, fateful, disclose
That oboe and flute, joining in, will review, and
    impressions convey...
A contest in ragtime with rivals a-blaring is headed our
    way.

Inventive capacity—ample—a couple of drummers will
    show.
Of feelings, not here but remembered, a painstaking
    cello will sing
While soft-pedaled chords on piano will hum to the
    friends in a ring.
The group reminisce, and emotions more deep and
    disturbing will grow.

204   ♫   *Martin Bidney*

'Tis better to tell of them well, unconcealing the lowliest
    thing.

A ludic fugato ensuing may unions astonishing wake:
Eleven musicians a single narration unanimous make.
The elegy (Ginsberg the patron, who'd praise, for a
    remedy, death)
Would gather, in gamelan spirit, all hewers and
    drawers of breath.
I, rather, a statement detect that affirms what the
    skeptic denies:
In you, English horn, will I trust for a love that can
    look to the skies.
Again comes the unison formed of what, scramble
    appearing to some,
Yet leads to the epilogue: Blest clarinet! For your
    kingdom is come.

9/1/19

91 Smetana

Bedřich Smetana
Má Vlast (first two movements of six)
Kyoto Symphony Orchestra, Uwe Mund
Notes by Oliver Kraft
Arte Nova Classics

Amphibrachic hexameter—first two strophes
x/x x/x x/x x/x x/x x/x
Dactylic hexameter catalectic—second two strophes
/xx /xx /xx /xx /xx /x

My Country!—I praise the idea—a man so attached to
    his homeland.
Though ruined the castle, impassioned the pained
    lamentation he's making,
High trumpeting heralds the life overlooking, outlasting
    the carnage—
A battle's recalled, re-enacted—yet pride and
    laudations are waking.

The conflict is fugally framed: neither nation nor man
    can forget it.
But life is the ultimate victor and, tone-creativity
    stirring,
We waking each day can renew the impulsion that life
    set in movement:
Like blossom and fruit on the tree are the forces of
    nature concurring.

Theme of the minstrel comes back in a blazon
    triumphal of glory.
Streams of the mighty Vltava, in rhythm of jig-time
    arising,
Childhood bring back: on a 78 rpm would the story
Well be conveyed, and the welling-up waters their
    task be emprising.

Days are a dance when the river at springtide the
    tempo determines;
Ought we attempt to see nymphs in the moonlight
    exultantly swimming?
Yes! and while gliding they'll even revisit the
    Vyšehrad palace.
River-theme (Hebrew Ha-Tíkvah) returns, and with
    bliss overbrimming.

9/2/19

92 Lalo

Édouard Lalo (1823–1892)
Symphonie Espagnole, op. 21
Itzhak Perlman, violin
Orchestre de Paris, Daniel Barenboim

Dactylic pentameter catalectic
/xx /xx /xx /xx /x

1

Roused to react, I will offer a sportscast to please you.
Opening theme isn't done when another one enters:
Then comes a third—is it possible? Had I mis-heard it?
No. When a fountain of melody wakes, we've a wonder
Meriting faithful account—let me try to provide it!

First theme is graced with abundant exactions athletic:
Second one—recognized, loved—cornucopial joyance.
Third of the melodies—friend and beloved companion.
Quick are the turning and twisting. Allegro non
        troppo?
Can't have "too much" of alacrity soul-overwhelming!

2

Here I am viewing a dance, and with gestures alluring.
Rapid the glad tarantella-type choreo-graphic:
Then come the intervals made for relaxed conversation—
Offering narrative rich in the life of her village.

Fiery the eyes—with the flappings of fan, and the
    stamping.

3

Triplet and duplet combine for a danceable ballad—
Fiddle and orchestra trading their phrasing-ideas
Till by a rapture excited, ecstatic possession
Has to take over awhile! When the seizure is ended—
Ah, looking back, by a tender caress are we
    vanquished...

4

Clouds—do they gather? A threatening storm is
    approaching.
Pauses, though brief, can disclose an unbearable
    burden....
Grieved, we present a memorial, rendering tribute.
Thoughts of the lately-so-youthfully-living have touched
    us:
Truly I feel and can see them—the tears of the people.

5

Dirge not yet ended—a rainbow appears in the heaven!
Soon comes the long-waited festival yearly occurring—
Raised with the copla, the bold solear, seguidilla,
Filled with the spirit of folksong and wit in our poems,
We, Violinist, your tune-theme and sweet variations

Love, both the fast and the slow—the rhapsodic, the
    gentle.
Fountain of Youth, you were sought by conquistador
    hikers,
Yet were you never discerned, I would claim, *till this
    minute*:
Raise up your arms to acclaim the supreme
    exsplendescent!
Praise be to God I have waited a lifetime to hear it!

9/2/19

93 Bloch

Ernst Bloch (1880–1959)
Prayer, Part I of the suite From Jewish Life, for cello
and piano,
The Jewish Soul
Amit Peled, cello, Eli Kalman, piano
Centaur

Dactylic pentameter catalectic
/xx /xx /xx /xx /x

Hearing this prayer—the cantor—the structure made
    subtle—
How to imprint on my memory all I am learning?—
Now that the cello's exploring a high obbligato,
Keyboard the tune will repeat, it will seem a bit
    clearer...

Second division—a spoken-like shaping, persuading.
Comes to assist me the opening statement, yet deeper.
Healing cadenza—Amen! at the end of the question.

Oh—I must play it again: let me concentrate harder.
Yes, I can chant it!—at least the whole opening section...
Even Part "B"—conversation—has come into focus.
"A"—then triumphant conclusion—reward for entreaty!

Lines from the Sabbatine psalms of King David recalling,
Maybe I'm meant to originate tunes for the Hebrew?
Silent I'll be—let the word, if I hear it, be welcomed.

9/2/19

94 Richard Strauss

Richard Strauss (1864–1949)
Das Rosenband
Songs by Sibelius, Strauss and Berg
Soile Isokoski, soprano, Marita Vitasalo, piano
Wigmore Hall Live, a BBC recording

*My Klopstock translation is in iambic tetrameter, first
and third lines masculine ending, second line feminine*
x/ x/ x/ x/
x/ x/ x/ x/x
x/ x/ x/ x/

*My own poem is in iambic pentameter, first and third
lines masculine rhymed, second line feminine*
x/ x/ x/ x/ x/
x/ x/ x/ x/ x/x
x/ x/ x/ x/ x/

*The Rose Wreath, Op. 36, No. 9 (1897)
by Friedrich Klopstock (1724–1803)*

*I found her in the springtime shade.
I bound her with a wreath of roses.
And unaware she slumbered on.*

*I looked at her. By this, my gaze,
My life and hers were blent together.
I felt it, though I knew it not.*

To her I whispered tonelessly
And rosy wreath I made to rustle.
    She from her sleep awakened then.

She looked at me. By this, her gaze,
Her life and mine were blent together.
    About us bloomed Elysium.

Rose Wreath Wordsong

Her staying quite asleep had made him sad.
The singer this with key change would betoken,
    Less vernal-toned than was the mood before.

Tranquillity returned for, thinking, glad,
That they were one in two, no link he'd broken:
    By this, the heart was nourished even more.

She gazed. A satisfaction deep he had:
Their mutual devotion, reawoken,
    Would let them chart a sea that has no shore.

9/2/19

95 Berg

Alban Berg (1885–1935)
Traumgekrönt
from Seven Early Songs (1905–1908, rev. 1928)
Soile Isokoski, soprano, Marita Vitasalo, piano
Wigmore Hall Live, a BBC recording

Iambic pentameters, tetrameter, dimeter
x/ x/ x/ x/ x/
x/ x/ x/ x/
x/ x/ x/ x/ x/
x/ x/

Dream-Crowned
by Rainer Maria Rilke (1875-1926)

That was the day of white chrysanthemums—
Their brilliance lent a vivid fright.
And then, to take my soul, a maiden comes
Deep in the night...

You—tender, gentle—came, though I was frightened.
My dream you'd graced with great delight.
And, as by tone of fairy-legend lightened,
Rang out the night.

Chrysanthemum Wordsong

Uncanny, wondrous... Wander we in dream
Till the beloved comes at last.

Then soft!—so mediation would beseem—
        All fears have passed.

The melody, continued as begun,
        Their gentle tread has deftly glassed.
Then suddenly—the singing nearly done—
        High tone! held fast!

9/2/19

96 Balákirev

Mily Balákirev (1837–1910)
Four Selections for Piano
Malcolm Binns Plays Balakirev, Pavilion Records

Dactyls in lines with varying beats: 8, 4, 7 (Islamey), 5
(Scherzo and Andantino), 5 and 6 (Mazurka)

1 Islamey

Start with a theme, orientally flavored, in rapidest
    triplets imaginable...
Building, legato, a flowing impelled by the motion of
    reverie water-inspired—
                Slowing the mood and the melody, full
                Of impatience to hear what will come
                    when required.
Bends in the river and spurting of current-
    deflections when rocks interfere
Lend inexhaustible motion, obsessive invention,
    propulsion, and cheer.

2 Scherzo No. 2

    Waterfall-waltz, in another deep dream of
        immersal—
    Suddenly halted—renewed, then a feeling-
        reversal:
    Thoughtful, a song, bringing rivulet triplets—a
        pause—

Rebel-percussion!—a mood with inscrutable
laws.
Legend-like tune, with the descant unendingly
flowing.
Oddly directionless—where is our reverie
going?

3 Andantino (from Sonata in B flat minor)

Soothing, a folk-theme turned fugal, then
stopped, and, rethinking
What it would do, it repeated the venture,
inquiring:
Maybe more passion? Unneeded, 'tis calm
we're desiring...
Streamlets of triplets take over, with rising and
sinking.

4 Mazurka (from Sonata in B flat minor)

Second beat always hit hard in a triple-time
dreaming,
Pleasant rubatos a jocular character adding.
Travel all over the keyboard, with pounding, or
skipping, or gleaming:
Tempos are getting more drunken, the spirit of
man to be gladding.

97 Sibelius

Jean Sibelius (1865–1957)
Tapiola, Op. 112
On CD 7 of Complete Collection
London Symphony Orchestra, Sir Colin Davis

Iambic pentameter
x/ x/ x/ x/ x/

A drum-crash, then—from song—a phrase recalled—
A warning prophecy? It happened twice...
The oboe frames another broken thought...
And all the while a long, low tone holds through.
Then, after uprush panicky and brief,
The violins take up the fragment-theme
In supple, curved, elaborated form,

And we are asked to think on it awhile
In higher and in lower tonal range...
In question, then in answer-form, until
The motive, that the woodwinds come to love,
And by the string group taken up in turn,
Arouse the brass to join awoken tones
That move the prime motif to be reshaped

In longer-floating formulation. Then—
A burst of strength disturbs the air. The rushed,
Disjointed duplets brave a testing flight.
The tiny, timid cries of little birds,
Then larger ones, more active mood create.

And now a pensive, baffled atmosphere
Must yield to force of what is coming on:

The theme that we began with plays a role...
A blast of trumpet, drum supported, starts
The third and final part of autumn's chant:
The maelstrom gathers energy and strength,
While the initial theme will try, with grace,
To reaffirm—but no!—huge random gusts!—
An after-calm, a waiting... whence uprise

The frightened birds that cover all the skies!
The leaves, atremble, high! a statement raise.
The onrush, the assault... will settle down.
We're left in quiet, as we'd been before.
The clamor, the tranquillity, the might
Have made a somber and a solemn psalm.

9/3/19

98 Buxtehude

Dieterich Buxtehude (ca. 1637–1707)
Aria: "La Capricciosa" in G Major, BuxWV 230
[in 32 parts]
Harpsichord Music Vol. 3
Lars Ulrik Mortensen

Ovidian dactylic hexameter distichs
/xx /xx /xx /xx /xx /x
/xx /xx /   /xx /xx /

Opening theme—not capricious, pre-Goldberg, majestic
    in measure—
Second appearance will fit, elegant, pleasant,
    serene.
Third we a "double" may call, with two eighth-notes
    each quarter replacing;
Fourth one the tune will divide, bass-line and
    treble between.

Sequences build on a scale in the fifth one, a rising
    and falling;
More of a rush in the sixth—boisterous, brusquely
    to run.
Seventh—we move even faster! while adding assertive
    expression.
Dotted the rhythms the eighth makes, to continue
    the fun.

Ninth comes alive with the triplets I dearly would love
    to be singing;

Tenth features quick-witted quip—four-quarter
time cut in threes.
Eight notes per utterance make our eleventh one swift
and affirming;
Twelfth is a game to display well-placed chromatics
at ease.

Luckiest number thirteen: superhuman in scale-
playing tempo.
Fourteen is restful and kind: question-and-answer
exchange.
Fifteen a love song might be, with some teasing and
hinting and whimsy;
Half of our piece to conclude, widely and rapidly
range!

Next, anachronic although it may be, on a railway I'm
riding.
Eighteen is equally swift—here with a bagpiper's
drone.
Nineteen—twelve-eight is the meter—a jig in a suite is
refreshing.
Twenty has moderate, firm, placid emotional tone.

Part twenty-one is a warm conversation, and lively in
content;
Song twenty-two could be used four-noted
groupings to teach.
Also an étude, most charmingly wrought, is the next
one—same tempo.
All limbered up? You're prepared jig-time perfection
to reach!

Tune twenty-five—you are ready to strum on the lute,
    con amore.
  Scales heading downward will lead, next, to a
    string-crossing feat
(Fiddlers would call it). In part twenty-seven, bright
    ornamentation,
  After a random attack, made resolution quite
    sweet.

Now we've a gaggle of sprightly inventions. An Irish-
    type folksong
  Nonstop proceeds to enjoy leapings in part twenty-
    nine.
Thirty the jig will be driving to left-hand vivace
    propulsion;
  Let all the countryside romp! Dancing's a *headier*
    wine!

Herald the festival shaped by agility, artful invention,
  Wisdom in relishing life, youth reassured in desire:
Part thirty-two will the march lend a steady
    advancement of gladness;
  Laud the left hand that can still kindle a sinistral
    fire!

9/3/19

99 Poulenc and Gervaise

Francis Poulenc (1899–1963)
Suite française d'après Claude Gervaise
pour violoncelle et piano (arr. Poulenc, 1939)
Francis Poulenc Oeuvres Complètes, disc 3
Erato

Trochaic octameter catalectic
/x /x /x /x /x /x /x /

Branslë de Bourgognë, to begin the sixteenth-century
Suite remade for modern hearers, charmingly appeals
    to me.
Stately, gentle-meditative, swims along the soft Pavane,
Liquefactive-limpid as the gliding of a water-swan,
Heart by dreaming scene to faded legendary kingdom
    drawn.

Little Military March—a happy child will smile, and
    move
Little men... The sudden end will lovably impulsive
    prove.
Plaint, a winsome lamentation, even stranger end will
    show:
Here the modern influence on olden song the plangent
    flow
Interrupts with mid-air chord a-dangle—where'd the
    dreaming go?

Branslë de Champagnë with a lullaby to start would
    seem:

Intervals of trouble come, yet theme recall with fairy-
    gleam.
Cradled shepherd-tempo, the Sicilian tune will calmly
    breathe,
Carillon bring back the mood of Christmas carol. We'll
    enwreathe
Festal ribbons 'round the swaddling garments that the
    baby sheathe.

9/4/19

100 Purcell

Henry Purcell (1659–1695)
Incidental Music to The Indian Queen
The Purcell Simfony and the Purcell Simfony Voices
Linn Records

Iambs in 7, 6, and 5 beat lines
Opening strophe:
x/ x/ x/ x/ x/ x/ x/

John Dryden, William Howard wrote a play, and yet
  we're not
Obliged to know what's happening, the annotator
  thought:
While incidental music we are learning, quite forgot
Will be the twisting-turning of the old heroic plot.
Sufficient, the delight that may with melodies be
  brought.
There's little risk—we'll try the disc, await the marvels
  wrought.

 In Overture let gentle and majestic be
 The opening, and then the hopping-skipping we
 Expected in the second part adorned we find
 With ornament-connectives, deft and well designed.
 (The Trumpet Tune, one minute, nicely is aligned.)

  When "Wake, Quivera" calls the singer, we
  Take pleasure in the dotted melody.
  The first five airs proceed at tranquil pace

Maintaining all the loved initial grace.
The summing-up duet takes grateful place.

Begins our Act the Second with a "symphony": the
    strings
Accompany the trumpet that, cajoling, smiling, sings
Till melancholy doom-invoking prospect supervenes...
A countervailing cheer, however, shuns dramatic
    scenes.
The chorus to a pacifying affirmation leans.

    Of flattery and envy forced to speak,
    The chanters, angry, castigate the weak.
    Three sequent instrumental works the ear
    Beguile—the playing so adept that we're
    Made thankful while the play is "rescued"
        here.

The creeping evils of the tensions that arise
One first laments, and then solution brave
    descries.
Chromatic, long ascent—the hero, pensive, broods
While consort, kind, of viols enters altered moods.
The duo-trumpets reassure us. Act the Third
At midpoint lets a bright auroral tune be heard.

While spirits of the air dispel imagined pain
And, canorous, the guides cry, "Languish not in
    vain,"
The trumpet and the viols offer stirring joys
To nourish hopes of men, when trying fate annoys.

'Tis melody lays low the bad dramatic ploys.
The tones a coming hidden harmony explain.

The single ayre that Act the Fourth presents
Five tunes will follow. Dolors, hie ye hence!

The Fifth and final Act, by placid chorus introduced,
As all before the sacred altar stand, the souls unloosed
From that which life would stifle, hail the glad
return
Of concord, and the dismal din of conflict spurn.

9/5/19

Notes

1. **Rameau.** I've been for years a habitual listener to keyboard suites or partitas by Bach and Handel, with movement types deriving from 18th century dance forms. It was Rameau who introduced me to a complementary French tradition with forms depicting mental states or moods (calm, agitated, angry, loving) or offering genre paintings of domestic or humanly affecting scenes. Compare **24 Milhaud** for a 20th century continuation of this Gallic tradition. **99 Poulenc / Gervaise** presents, in the film music where a 20th century composer builds on the work of a 16th century master, a hybrid or compromise of the two traditions. The two "bransle" dances (our word "brawl" derives from this beautiful word, with the "s" unpronounced) are picturesquely given regional origins; the "sicilienne" is a standard kind of melody-form, but with a memory of shepherd idylls (as when the shepherds watch their flocks by night in Handel's *The Messiah*); "pavane" is a dance while "complainte" is a mood.

2. **Moszkowski.** An internationally influenced German Jewish composer, Moszkowski wrote music filled with flowing movement that made me want to shape a verbal gondola-song. Flow is the pre-eminent quality of all the movements I heard; and the same is true of all the music I surveyed before writing **96 Balákirev.**

3. Prokofiev. Juxtaposing, from a Prokofiev duo sonata for violins, the two movements I liked best, I chose to offer them as two stages in a life. What I am after—always, primarily—in these wordsongs is to shape a work of art based on what the music of the given composer has meant for me, in my own reverie world, at a chosen moment of intro- and retrospection. No claims are ever made to have distilled the essence, or to have summed up the typical traits, of any composer's writing. Here is Prokofiev heard in another mood:

Sergei Prokofiev: A Sonnet
5/6/06

His weaving deviations from the key
In the beloved *Romeo* ballet,
First violin concerto, witty play
Of Kijé, or the *Classic Symphony*

Will turn the sweetest lyricism we
Might think we ever heard to what a strange
Disorienting dance!—where all may change
To fairy tale *bylína*, crazily—

With frequent humor. In a string quartet
I heard sarcastic jokes that, pointed, cut.
"Scythian" rhythm can be brutal. But
The rural tuneful music that he set

For balalaikas and for tambourines
In *Romeo* shaped warm folkloric scenes.

4 Scarlatti. Another hearing of an endlessly inventive melodist:

Eteri Andjaparidze Playing Scarlatti
(11/17/12)

Surprise and game and little phrase
To echo, jumping rope on days
Each one as long as later on
A week might be—or with amaze

Caress the cat more soft than lawn,
Asparkle off the fur-tips: gone
A mood? Well, soon—no wait—replaced
With quick-planned leap. The moment-spawn

Of impulse, we—no whim erased
And what is coming pleasing-paced—
And loud I sing if so the god
Be pleased to want. When swinging-spaced,

The hours are counted by the nod
Of up and down, and sky and sod,
And forth and back, the rhythm-ways
Of warmth and wind, of play and laze.

5. Evening Robin. The length of bird call phrases reminded me of the varied length and shape of a number of cantillation neumes or tropes used in Hebrew Bible recitation and learned in the passage required to be chanted on my Bar Mitzvah celebration at age 13—a mode of musical declaiming widely acknowledged to have decisively influenced the Gregorian Chant:

The Lover's Morning Service

The birds in cantillation tropes
Upon their torah scroll, the sky—
Merkháh tupkháh in rapid cry—
Will write their bright arising hopes.

The chanter's unregarding of
A neighbor-reader muttering.
His impulse to the winds to fling
Is high command of humble love.

Khayeï olám, the life eterne,
Natá', He planted, startlingly,
Where? *Be-tokheïnu*—in us all.

We sing it in our longing call,
We know it, and the soul will yearn,
We *are* it, and the heart is free.

Here I wish to be Shulamith-muse to the Solomonic robin:

First Robin
(4/1/13)

The showers that the Venus-time of April brings
Can not perturb the robin looking for the worms
That might emerge from hedge-base puddle when the rings
Of plopping drops outripple. He, so near, confirms

With gules of heraldry on bright-outswelling breast
The role of crier of the Solomonic news
That made me love the shiver that might shake my rest,
Old sluggard-ways remaining. Fail not, Shula-muse,

To shape a tune made worthy of the prophet-will
Of this returning friend, who's come to emblemize
The meeting and the mating of the winter chill
With singing-drive and yearning, spurring vernal sighs.

Listen to a few more birds—I write about my sun-prophets
with great pleasure:

Birds
(5/12/08)

(1)

The bird outside my window here,
A healer and a paraclete,
Whose mood-improving tune replete
With life untiring, chirruped cheer

In function cannot but endear,
A herald that has come to greet
In flame-tongue pentecostal, clear
As—bright!—the tiding of a sweet

New eden, triller-paradise
In rillet-whirl and turn and chirr,
A heart-enlarging harbinger

New-brightening the widened eyes
Of one whom day can yet surprise
An "angel" is, a "messenger."

(2)

A bird, whose punctuated call
Begins with double downward slide,
Then big, fresh liquid burst—in all
A dozen one-pitch notes—to glide

Right by my ample window which
Has formed a clear transparent wall
That's letting penetrate the rich
Tones that on grateful ear will fall,

Is thinking for a moment. Stirred,
I write my thank-you word to it,
Until another singer flit

Into the wide and open yard
To let another hymn be heard:
One is the heart of bird and bard.

More about Birds
(5/13/11)

More steady than the dark, the chill,
Their unabated living skill
Most fortified before the morn...
Best heaven-effort, never still,

A mate to gain, a male to warn:
Bright will, a myriad times reborn
Though void of sign of rhodal dawn,
Both love to praise and foe to scorn.

Why love and war in dark to spawn?
We want to think they carry on
Their psalming with a hope that grows,
A fierce and piercing marathon

Of affirmation while the rose,
To mercy-dew replying, glows
In aromatic passion... Will
Our dream be proved? God only knows.

The Birds Return
(5/14/11)

When Oscar Wilde compared a princess' laughing to
The sound of water from a silver pitcher poured,

He gave a sense of what a happy lilting through
A quiet, sudden, brings of glory-light restored.

So inexhaustible and strong, the more-and-more'd
Insisting of a thousand callings out to You!
Who is the addressee? Can we the seeker view?
How can the coming flood requite the ocean-oared?

O energy of wealth each beggar may afford
To shower down to ground, a Zeus of music true!
Deep Danaë, come forth, and hear what he'll bestrew

Of tributaries that accumulate in blue:
Sing, choral group of males, your tale of yearning horde
Of Horus, lord aborning, soaring in accord!

Let's close with two more birds:

Die Nachtigall, sie war entfernt: Goethe's Nightingale, My Robin
5/27/06

The nightingale had gone away.
He's back again, for spring.
He trilled the same old songs today,
He hasn't learned a thing.

"Singt alte liebe Lieder," Goethe said
Of that much-fabled bird, the nightingale.
No need for new, the favorites won't fail.
"Sings all the golden oldies." Lieder-led,

I store, absorb, the poured-out silver-pure
And canorous *concerti* in my head:
Piccolo soloist, the robin red
Completes the wood wind suite the overture

With morning-glory color introduced
Even before the dawn rose in reply.
Talking with neighbors, to the music I
Listen and learn the latest news, am loosed

From cold, contracting exiguities—
Old imposition of the winter freeze.

    6. Couperin. The effect of this profound composer's work
upon my music-life is great, especially of his *Leçons de
Ténèbres:*

The Ninth of Av
(7/28/12)

The floor is carpeted, so crying candles left
Not only marks but wax embedded, hard to clean.
That used to happen. Now, by flashlight will be seen
The text to read of how the temple fell. Bereft

And weeping, She who was the radiant, sacred queen,
Princeps provinciarum—vidua—the word
Of Lamentations coming back, with music heard
In *Lessons of the Dark* by Couperin. Between

The Jewish and the Catholic laments no cleft
Is felt by me when chants are blent, by dark bestirred
To sigh for all the arson, carnage that occurred

When bestial blindness rent aside the holy weft
Adorned, before the ark, with cherub and with palm.
It happens now, ev'n as we chant in darkened calm.

    7. Koerner. My ears are attuned to poetic meters of
striking kinds whenever they occur in the midst of prose.
Another case in point:

Afflatus
(1/3/06)

Addiction? Yes. Benign? I'm hoping so.
"Tormentuous in combativity"—
I heard the words; they made a mark in me.
I had to write them down, or they would grow

Too great, or sadder yet, they'd simply go
For good, a fine pentameter be lost.
Iatric iambs impiously tossed
Away are unforgiven, since we know

The gifts the gods benignantly bestow
Must actively be handled and apprised.
They come when I would never have surmised.
To cheer, to sing *in dulce jubilo*—

That is the right reaction. I'll not fear
A sonnet seizure. I will hold it dear.

    A jaunty word rhythm is a vitamin tonic. One more case
in point:

Pills to Purge Melancholy
sonnet-variant with dactyls
(5/12/06)

Multiple harmony supplement, rhythm-enriched,
Threefold the strength of the usual tunes you have heard—
    Suddenly stirred,
Wouldn't you find metabolic activity pitched

Higher, more rapidly vitaminized when you drank
In, through the ear, what would hardly have entered before?
    Open the door.
Meter transmogrifies mind. You will cordially thank

Fortified heartbeat enhancement that's mightier still:
Triple syllabic solutions accelerate. Air
    Circulates there,
Grandly expanding the mind and restoring the will.

    Try it today.
Many, the metrical messages heading your way!

I was further alerted to the alliance of metric form with prose eloquence when my late friend Peter Bridge—composer, pianist, and retired Librarian of Congress who had retired to live in my home town of Vestal NY— told me that Cicero (often called Tully in Britain) climaxed orations with phrasings that were shaped by Vergilian meter.

Peter had a composer's ear for musical tactics. He loved to sight-read adventurously with me. Here's a record of a session we had:

Sight-reading with Peter Bridge: A Sonnet
(8/10/06)

Seven sonatas in an afternoon.
Handel—did he invent the *allargando*?
Corelli's minor-ending jig will soon
Strangely fade out, will soften, a *calando*.

The E flat Bach sonata for the flute—
Queenly, serene, a greening in the spring.
The B flat Mozart, clever and astute—
Tender, invention endless, frolicking.

A couple of Corellis, Bachs, and now:
Cool stream cascading in a torrent swift.
Young Mendelssohn—his nature taught him how
To praise: brave adolescent lyric lift.

I am the same fine animal as they,
Livened and heightened by the hymns I play.

I feel most like a composer when I'm writing a wordsong of the kind I playfully call "song without words." That means simply that whatever discursive meaning the piece may have, its main satisfaction and deepest joy come from the alliterations and assonances, the harmonies of consonants and of vowels. Here's one of many I've written:

Sonnet Without Words
(6/4/06)

Discouragers incur an angel ire.
Approval and applause are merited
Whenever, impulse entering the head,
Schooled in the love of craft, the tyger fire,

Exuberance, along the neural wire,
Enlivening the mind to make the said
More lovely for the way of saying, led
To elevate the lowly on the lyre,

And able so, by singing, to acquire
A lucency, release, a lightness fed
Right from the heart's own primal fountainhead
From whence alone arising, our desire

Fled, will affirm the high, the fearless flier,
Flaming and free, a heaven-life, or higher.

8. Tchaikovsky. This composer has been a big part of my life for a very long while. I listened to his symphonies 4, 5, and 6 dozens of times apiece. Whenever he comes up again I'm glad: here I present him transvaluating the famous three-note "fate" theme that opens Beethoven's *Symphony No. 5.*

A gray and drippy morning of early June
(6/6/17)

A gray and drippy morning of early June
Would soon be lightened while, in a long massage,
    The muscle fiber tension devils
  Learned they'd be cudgeled away forever.

Returned, I found a treat: the computer screen
Revealed plump berries gathered from Sarah's yard.
    (The time is ripe—for Minnesota.)
  This I would mail to my friends—a present.

Next, brunch (delayed) for one who's forbidden jam:
Ezekiel toast and pesto with pine-nuts mild
    We top with fiery pickled mango,
  Sent to me here from an Indian village.

My kitchen I with foods of a world away
Can fill: the *saag* or spinach and mustard greens,
    The *dal* of lentils, onion, eggplant—
  Save me the fare of the airplane travel.

The radio's beginning the final part
Of that Tchaikovsky symphony most admired
    By me, who loved it back in high school:
  Only the Fifth had a sudden breakthrough—

A theme in unrelentingly minor mode
Would—silenced—yield to marching in triple time
    That led the mood-swing transformation
  Turning our journey to manic gladness.

We melancholy anguish, a burden, learned...
That fate is molten down by the newly freed!

A four-note bang on hammered anvil—
Beethoven beat! *And the Fifth we answer!*

9. Glazunov. When the Binghamton Community Symphony Orchestra, Tim Perry conducting, performed "Autumn" here last fall, a door was opened for me into *The Seasons*, another masterwork by Glazunov.

10. Telemann. I zeroed in on the party theme in this composer's writing, for I played one of his many entertaining violin movements at the Indiana University High School 1960 graduating class reunion, along with Handel and some Irish and Scottish folk music. Here's an e-mail poem relating to that festal event:

Response to an Article: Thank You for Posting It, Dave!
(9/2/11)

Reunion-time, as here described, is really fun.
Although I cannot go to our November one,
It's great to feel the joy the present writer shared
With someone else who to a fine reunion fared.

He had to shout above the music? Much too loud.
But I in high school knew a more melodious crowd.
Neanderthudding sixties? Better forties, fifties:
I loved the golden oldies, plus the newer nifties.

But let me note, as well, what century I mean:
Before the fifty, forty, write a *seventeen*!
Vivaldi, Bach, Corelli, Mozart, Telemann
Are with me every day and never will be gone.

Restarting varied harmony again today,
Let tunes recharm the heart, our better angels play.

Telemann, I think, is hugely underestimated. Here's another write-up of mine, where I had hoped to evoke his

elegant wealth of melody by using the exuberant alcaic meter
borrowed from ancient Rome:

Four Telemann cantatas—I felt an ease
(5/28/17)

Four Telemann cantatas—I felt an ease
When thinking, these one might have performed at home
    With music-minded friends invited:
  So the "soirées" that we held in high school—

We called them that, it had such a grownup sound—
Let gentle charm post-prandial mood improve.
    The Music Master: *Cecidērunt,*
  Though *in profundum* the scale went downward,

Could not dismay, for sprightlier wit was king.
The *allerschönsten Lippen* would love deny
    Yet failed in that attempt. A lover
  Can't be rejected when love's within him.

By funeral lament for a bird that died
We might be saddened, yet with returning spring...
    Predictable, our reassurance:
  Briefly bemused we enjoy what's tuneful.

Die Hoffnung ist mein Leben—my life is hope.
Philosophy concludes what we knew before:
    The grace of happy chymic humor
  Never will fail you for entertainment.

11. Ysaÿe. I had the rare privilege of hearing a series of
contemporary music recitals given in his later years by violinist
Josef Szigeti, resident artist at the Indiana University School
of Music in Bloomington, Indiana where I grew up.

12. Shostakovitch. His Fifth Symphony was an anthem of freedom to us the 1950s and '60s. Through the years I have come to appreciate him ever more deeply: the preludes and fugues made him, for me, the Russian Bach.

The nineteen-nine concerto for cello proves
(6/3/17)

The nineteen-nine concerto for cello proves
Not grand, romantic—rather, novella-swift.
  The fated theme, our hero's name-card:
  Four-note obsession of Shostakovitch.

'Tis manic agitation, a kind of cheer
Infected by depression, the folk-motif
  Despairing, daring, through the city,
  Fleeing with glee from a nightmare mindset.

More soft than mother's lullaby comes the tune
Of cello with an oboe in counterpoint:
  When clarinet takes up the crooning,
  Solo will switch to an obbligato.

The song is calming, mutedly tearful, too,
Until in dream-harmonics away it drifts
  To blend with heavenly celesta:
  Overcoat-reverie, Gogol-story.

No swaggery cadenza from early time:
Soliloquy, instead, of a Hamlet-depth.
  Dull, sullen wrath is ugly, sulky,
  Then is enraged by the theme returning.

Prophetic, that—for next with pogróm-like threat
The signature of doom on the sky will blaze:
  The folk motif—an army marching.
  Thuggish, the crowds, and their numbers matter.

Here is another brief sketch, noting the viola-piano sonata and the Tenth Symphony:

Dmitri Shostakovitch
on a charcoal drawing of him by Aubrey Schwartz
(3/26/06)

Dramatic lyric of soliloquies:
A meditative Hamlet in the first
Viola declamation, then a burst
Of drunk, lopsided Gogol humor. These

Are but the starting incongruities:
Now the viola, homeless on the heath,
Wandering, lives for "Moonlight," scattered wreath,
Loose moods and leaves, remembered mysteries.

A prelude, fugue, in their nobility
Are like a testament. Tenth Symphony:
Here is a pilgrimage, where D.-Es-C.-
H. is the theme. The song-biography

Ends in a fragile triumph—hope reborn—
'Twill blend sad signature with *wunderhorn.*

13. Ives. To the most wildly inventive, and from my point of view the most rewarding, American composer of the late 19th and early 20th century (commended by e.g. Schoenberg for inventive ingenuity) I composed this tribute-sonnet in a vaguely Gertrude Steinian style:

Charles Ives
(1/3/07)

Atrample grand old gramps and grandmas grammar
Aslant and hanging tantrum slambrash blunder

Standing a thicket crash a thrashing under
Autumnal sun a fallen branchbang hammer

No bar but thunder violin ascurry
More drum drum silence final final drum
Is it the quiet will the heart schlag come
Quail call or apoplectic leafmeal flurry

Mournful a warning echo family
Polyphony a flute and oboe strings
Pound pound piano drummer left hand flings

A notice vauntlet violining pain
Tremolo crying die die die again
O fount of every blessing where the key

One of the most thrilling events of my life was, after a year
of rehearsal in preparation, to play with Asher Raboy in the
Casadesus Hall at Binghamton University a recital that
included Ives' magnificent Sonata No. 2 for violin and piano,
which blended elements of square dance, jig, ragtime, hymn
and other American forms with Ives' own incomparable
conjurations:

Happy Heptameters for Libby Tucker
(8/21/12)

A splendor-making summer has it been, friend Libby. Too,
I hope to hear of sunny mental weather sent to you.
The nightingale and rose will aid the Persian verser: we
Are sheltered by what cricket-chirp the year can echo
        through.

My Goethe-verse, anew remade, was on the BBC
For hearers offered recently in recitations three.
The *Goethe Yearbook* favored me: how grateful the review!

244 ♩ Martin Bidney

There breathed within a synthesis a vineyard symphony.

The concert that I played at forty-one I now pursue
Re-mastered on my website: Schumann, Bloch, and Ives, a
    few
Companions on a pilgrimage who drunk revealed to me
What vernal birds might prophesy that azure-gold foreknew.

A nidifice patration will awake infinity:
Of winds primifluous the roblet omniregency,
Ethereal idea riviation aiding, flew
To meet the need of ramifactive action speedily.

14. Bidney. My debut as a singer/songwriter employed texts from the book I co-wrote with German poet and scholar Philipp Restetzki, *Ein nie geahntes Vergnügen / A Treat Not Known Before: Deutsche-Amerikanische Poetische Dialoge in alten Rhythmen / German-American Poetic Dialogues in Ancient Rhythms* (Dialogic Poetry Press: Vestal NY, 2017, available on Amazon). My friend Venkatesh Balasubramanian has transferred to computer software, and also added guitar chords to, the 14 songs I have composed in ancient Greco-Roman meters. I plan to publish these within the year, *deo volente aut musa volante.*

15. Copland. The opening line refers to Charles Ives' "The Unanswered Question," where the trumpet questions while the strings, oblivious, dream. I've written more than one tribute to the Master of the Appalachian Spring:

Aaron Copland
(12/15/05)

Thanks! for the towering Third Symphony,
A work I never tire of. You can hear
The fourth- and fifth-based harmonies, endear-
ing, bold, and mighty. There, the monody

To Lincoln is implied—and, too, the Fan-
fare loved so well. Friend Copland, Jew, and gay,
Wrote of an Appalachian spring. The way
He did it—as a great inventor can—

Was to acquire the folk anthology
Compiled by Alan Lomax, then create
A spare and primal-sounding chordwork. Fate
Brought from Vitebsk a mind that wandered free

With Shakers and Stravinsky—zigzag path,
Playful—a rootless cosmopolymath.

And here a stirring meditation by the composer blends
with the rest of an evening in my life:

Copland's Third Symphony on the Radio at Home
(5/30/11)

A crisis in the building of a nation
Succeeded "Fanfare of the Common Man"—
A block: no concept came for the formation
Of ways to complement the fathers' plan.

A one-note bird alone his call repeating
Confronted prophets of decline and fall:
He's joined by more, a joyous choral greeting
To lend men strength when horns' determined call

Fills out the pattern practiced in the chanteys
That started up the heart, as after rain—
Which, by the way, is pouring down again!

The thunder-dancing of the corybantes
With clashing of the armor, spears, and shields,
To greet— each night!—Cybele chaos wields.

Have you heard Copland's settings of poems by Emily Dickinson? They impressed me:

A Thank-You Sonnet for Bruce Borton
(11/11/07)

Easy to comprehend why Robert Frost,
Flushed with the pride and heightening that far
Bettered the mild "Choose Something Like a Star,"
Should yell, "Sing that again!" No feeling lost

In Randall Thompson's warm rendition, all
Was grand enhancement, even setting right
The bad "It aSkS of uS a Certain height"—
Sibilants that the Sybil would appal.

"Song of Democracy"—here, even more,
The Howard Hanson melody would pour
A fiery and a fuller-bodied wine.

And Copland brought out well the misery
Hiding behind the riddles of E. D.—
Doubling the dolor of each valued line.

16. Schubert. Responding to the Philip Friedheim Memorial Presentation including a performance by pianist Michael Salmirs and baritone Timothy Lefebvre and a lecture by musicologist Harry Lincoln in Casadesus Hall at Binghamton University, I wrote the following sonnet:

Response to the Goethe-Schubert "Erlkönig"
for Tim Lefebvre, Michael Salmirs, Harry Lincoln
(9/19/08)

"Den Erlenkönig," "Alder King," he fears—
Rushing in whistling wind and rustling leaves.

The father "reasons," but the boy believes:
The innocent an evil spirit hears.

What hooded horror in the wood! Strong seers
Feel, cold, the chaos-demon that bereaves:
Yet one lost waif in living legend grieves
More than grave Dante in dead midlife years,

Foul-tree-surrounded, foundered in the wild.
There is no soul that will not be a child,
Alone and shaking, weak in bone-chill night,

To see no minding sign in shrouded light,
Enhearsing hope, lest fevered shout be heard—
The darker scream-beast by the heart bestirred.

This relates to an earlier invoking of the Schubert setting, which I had mailed to a friend:

The Alder King
answering a question from Johanna Masters
(2/24/08)

"Erl-König" is the Alder King
    Who snatched the seër child
In Schubert's rumble-thundering
    Setting of Goethe's wild

And gripping and tormenting tale.
    The grisly forest force
Whirls the dear boy away in wail
    Of wind: the wildered horse—

Embrangled anguish in the gleams
    Of wide-eyed bloody gaze—
On through the branching tangle streams,
    Shattering, in a daze.

And what then of the horrid woe
    The father had, the fit
That seized his trampled spirit so?
    I cannot speak of it...

There is no greater tragedy
    Than for a child to die.
What deeps of seething jealousy
    In Death's fell venom lie!

And here's a more easygoing set of reverie-impressions in quite a different mood:

Schubert Impromptus
played by Vladimir Horowitz
(5/27/13)

Not-prompted, feeling free, and yet
In classic shape symmetric set,
They start with ABA, the mold
That, rhetoricians tell, may let

An artful argument unfold:
Expound, elaborate, then hold
The first assertion up to view
To cap, to sum the story told.

The rondo form's familiar, too:
ABACA. Here may you
Recall sonatas' fast-slow-fast,
The three-part talk now five-part. Few

The changes made by Schubert: past
Tradition knew when moods contrást
We're happier, for life is bet
And risk and chance and calm at last.

The slow and solemn marching rhythm in the unforgettable Allegretto of Beethoven's Seventh found adequate spiritual reply in a Schubert song, employed as theme of transcendent string quartet variations that I had a chance to play (both second and first violin, on different occasions) in eighth grade and high school:

Beethoven's *Allegretto*, Schubert's *Death and the Maiden*
for Louise Fairfax
(11/14/07)

The second movement of the Seventh Symphony—
Quarter, two eighths, two quarters (one motivic bar)—
A *maestoso*, but with lightness from afar,
A solemn walk, sigh ending, hymnlike too, for me

Will often bring to mind the Schubert melody
"Death and the Maiden" where the anapest will star:
Hear we the tread of death? Where the eternal are
The somber Mother and her springtime child may be

At one in lightness that our grieving will dissolve.
Most tender *allegretto* that can so involve
The deep-relentless with a counterpoint of cries

And height! We feel the march of every human fate
No mere procession but progression. Dedicate
Your walk of life to what your *daimon* will devise.

And, lastly, there came to me something like an epitaph:

Franz Schubert: A Sonnet
(3/17/06)

Free dreamer, chronicler of mental weather,
Hard-writing, syphilitic, rarely tragic,

All sadness merged within a lyric magic,
Eyes widened, childlike, grave and gay together,

He dream-time gave a newly ample space.
Exalted startling heart-stop harmonies
Come unaccountably. Dance-monodies
Incorporate spring thunder, with a grace

That lends the late piano works a pull
More deep than tears. He blends the never-slowing
Waters the miller hears with onward flowing
Stream of desire. The winter-walker, full

Of death-directed pensive poetry,
Turns bitterness to wisdom—even he.

17. Cowell. Lines 1 and 3 allude to the Islamic description of God as "Cleaver of the Daybreak" (Qur'an 6:95).

18. Schoenberg. Here I enjoy another of his retrospective wonders:

Schoenberg for Profit and Pleasure
a sonnet for my late friend Tom Head
(11/22/15)

A suite: piano, woodwinds three, and add three strings,
The opus twenty-nine's my comfort music now:
The Dance-Steps, Overture, Jig, Variations make
The strangest-yet kaleidoscope of the baroque.

So Shostakovitch in each fugue and prelude brings
Wise Bach alive again; Ravel's tombeaux allow
An eighteenth-century impressionist to wake;
Respighi dance and air may charm us modern folk.

A week of daily playings hadn't dulled the suite,

Which as a ready friend my leisure glad will greet.
For ingenuity he won't take second place

To brave and wild Stravinsky. Delicacy, grace,
With no more vigor-storm than tenderness will bless
The ardent lovers of this wit and heart-largesse.

19. Hindemith. Closely related is another poem I wrote, also containing elements of memory-flashback intertwined with those of present-day contemplation:

Hindemith's "Kammermusik"
for Anni
(9/29/12)

A little song that never faded but would stay
And faithful entertain me gaily on the way
From out the suite where it appeared in junior high
To show me how to wander, confident the play

Of choice, annoyance, joy, and boisterous aplomb
Would comfortingly to familiar keynote come,
Returned. I heard the weeping century go by:
Stravinsky village-weird, Pierrot alone and glum,

The Russian roughness, and the wilds of Ives, the drum
Of Shostakovitch Fifth, and yet the quirky, fey
(Which means a manic, antic mood when doomed to die)
Entwined with contrapuntal wonder that would say

The brain will take the road above, and halidom
Awake in governing the passion-avid clay,
That fate might have a tearful humor in her eye,
And heartstring tremble when a glance will feather-strum.

Ten years ago, I felt like this:

Hindemith Conducts Hindemith: A Couplet Sonnet
EMI CD of some orchestral works
(8/15/09)

The man's piano works will often be
Nostalgia-trapped, abandoned elegy,
Yet concert music made for brass and strings,
The Suite from "Noble Vision," sterner things
And stronger, and more epic-centered, live
By sage deliberation, which may give
A dignity to sadness, while they lend
Narration-depth: beginning, middle, end.

The consequence of an assertion draw
With long-devoted soul, and you will awe
The logic-heart that traces out the tale
Of contrapuntal walking through our vale
Of war and sorrow, and of light and drive—
Strange melody—to keep the mind alive.

And here, from a dozen years back, is my initial impression
of the masterwork treated in **19 Hindemith**:

Hindemith's "Concerto for Orchestra": A Sonnet
(12/3/07)

The twittering and crowing of a waking forest—
That is the ordered, choiring jumble: oboe, horn,
Bassoon and flute are beast and bird, a squirrel morn
The tireless violin. Fast, uncontrolled, they've morrised,

And in between, the boughs and massy winds have
    chorused
A theme that in the brain of Bach, we bet, was born,
Whose heavy emphasis the creatures might forewarn:
Cloudburst, and thunder drumbeat! Ample allegórist,

The slower-mooded young composer's measured calm
In hymn-processional, majestic, brings a balm,
The dotted rhythm and the undetermined key

Leading to odd impromptus unexpectedly,
Which, integrated with our march when it resumes,
Add lilt and lift. But look: another tempest looms.

Incidentally, my late friend the composer and pianist Peter Bridge considered Hindemith his chief mentor as inventive music-maker, a deep affinity to which I paid tribute in the following:

A Parallel
*sonnet after a music session
with pianist-composer Peter Bridge*

To sight-read Hindemith—why not?—right through
The violin-piano so-called E
Sonata, as we did successfully
This afternoon, can readily renew

Enamoring and glad complexity.
Prankish professor, might he be like you?
Plays by the contrapuntal rules, but few
The stable bases in the elegy.

Whimsical divagations, yet the clue
Never withheld for long, providing we,
By hemiolas and a lack of key
Remain unfazed, relish the ranging view.

Glenn Gould would play and mirror him—a free
Lunar Pierrot of the piano, he.

20. Stephen Foster. Here's another fond childhood memory of the man:

Of the longed-for and gone Swanee River we sang
a memoir poem
(10/8/18)

Of the longed-for and gone Swanee River we sang
    And, nostalgic, the child-trebles rang.
I developed a liking for Foster, and soon
    His biography read, blessèd boon.

I would learn that the "Swanee," that canorous name,
    Only doubtful distinction might claim.
Many alternate options in vain had been tried:
    "Down the Yazoo" (!) all beauty defied...

But the lulling Sewanee, three-syllabled stream,
    Both the tune and the mood would beseem.
"Let us all mispronounce it," the arbiter said,
    And no further would trouble his head.

When the spirit appears, knee the pedant must bend,
    Tip his hat, and due homage extend.
Generations of children—they'd have to be taught
    Something novel that Foster begot.

For the somnolent Swanee, that melody-swan—
    Here a moral perhaps can be drawn—
With a second-best choice proving better than none,
    Better finish what once you've begun.

Apropos of the annual Dulcimer Gatherings I mention in poem 20, here's another unforgettable sweet memory. (Maybe I should add: the title refers to the dulcimer-playing maiden seen by Coleridge in his "Kubla Khan," one of my favorite poems for as long as I can remember liking poems.)

Damsel
(8/25/16)

On tenor dulcimer the bow
When drawn gets tone with swelling might.
The plucked ones—lyric, vocal, bright—
Would shimmer, complement the low.

The folk-crowd loved the dulcy show.
My fiddle—unexpected sight.
Their sounds to me seemed benedight,
I, friendly, wished to blend! And so:

Informal consort, willing wight...
It was a "happy birthday!" glow
The fiddle made, she let me know—

And kissed me. Yes, you read that right!
A blest and elegant delight
I sudden felt, so long ago.

21. O'Carolan. I included selections from this redoubtable, itinerant Irish harp minstrel and composer in the violin music offered to my friends from the Class of 1960, Indiana University High School, in a 50th reunion concert I gave:

Meter, mood, even pitch compete
(5/18/19)

Meter, mood, even pitch compete:
Time to utter some praise, loud, to the engineer,
Videographer, schoolmates, all
Who on YouTube a gift rendered: accept my thanks!

When I first had begun my song,
Tunes were running around, still, in my wakened brain:

Handel, Telemann, Cárolán—
Strange "Lord Moira" strathspey—then, in a bluegrass mode

(Scottish forebear of this, at least),
"Miss Jane Cooper," the reel aided by Wanda's dance!—
"Baptist Johnston," a folk jig named
After someone who shared food with a minstrel blind.

Now they've gone for awhile, and I
Write to you in a form, old, with a brand-new beat.
Read the ditty aloud—you'll note
How the singable words dance in your mind at once!

Prosper, flourish, and happy years
Many more may you spend, Univee friends of mine!
Let the spirit of cheer abound,
Sounding into the height, Bloomington, much-loved home!

Here's another time when I played O'Carolan:

After-Party Thoughts
an amphibrachic jig
(3/18/12)

St. Patrick's Day: "Lark in the Morning" I played,
And then "Sheebag Sheemore," the quick and the slow;
For fast, "Baptist Johnston": an end to the show
"O'Carolan's Quarrel with Landlady" made.

The deck at the back of the house had been laved
In sunlight that mildly the breeze had caressed:
I cheerfully fiddled, was feeling my best,
And poured out the joy-of-the-springtime I'd saved.

No matter what vigor my bow would expend
Affirming a friendliness weather-confirmed,

Within me, suppressed, an aversion had squirmed:
The bark of the dog getting louder—no end

To bellowing—sharply discharged as a gun,
The yowls each relentless, repeated, intense!
Oblivious, filled with a passion immense,
I blacked it all out: I would rival the sun!

Some claimed that the clapping excited the beast;
Or maybe he somehow felt threatened? At best,
I rose to the challenge and, passing the test,
I felt I'd been singing the springtime, at least.

A sickening residue stayed with me, though:
What happened to honor—and plain self-regard?
Unthinking self punishment? It had been hard
Resisting that mad adversarial woe...

Self-humbled, insulted? A failure of heart?
Yet why should resentment be wiser? And why
Regret, and why shame? Shallow vanity, fie!
I'd entered a moment emblazoned with art.

Wouldn't you love to hear just a little more about that quarrel
with the landlady? O'Carolan himself wrote a song about it,
and here's my song about that song.

"O'Carolan's Quarrel with His Landlady"
a song for music
(3/20/07)

Landlady and O'Carolan:
The title plainly claimed they fight.
Music disproved it, made to scan
Movingly. Dark, now light,

Windily, moods their whim-race ran.
Now tears, now triumph came to sight,
Now separate, now blended. Can
Love show a higher might?

They do not merely "quarrel." Fan
The fire awhile, and then it's right
Parting and simple grief the man
May sadden in the night.

Music, enlarge our mortal span,
Our heartbeat hasten, making bright
A climbing flame. What love began
Raise to a later height.

And maybe you'd enjoy a sonnet in Hibernian-style dactylic
jig-time?

"Maggie Brown's Favorite": Irish Folk Jig Sonnet
7/27/06

Steadily venturing—simple, habitual—
Bland, undemanding, though handily danceable—
Melody mellow and mildly enhanceable—
Planned, unelaborate rhythmical ritual—

Feeling of galloping, prancing, and cantering—
Triple-time fiddling to cheer you relaxingly:
Festive, equestrian, gently—untaxingly—
Rapidly chanting and happily bantering.

Presently, then, what was pleasantly pillowing
Confident calm, a predictable, merrily
Singable thing became crazily, scarily
Swaying and raving, a breaker-wave billowing—

Rearing and rising!—then sinking, subsiding.
Fine!—I survived it, inspired by the riding.

22. Romanian Folk Music. My parents' families came
from Lithuania and Ukraine, and I'm attracted to Americans'
memoirs of life in Eastern and Central Europe:

Romanian-American Thoughts on "A Fence with a Gate"
to Andrei Guruianu, with gratitude for his lyric prose
(8/16/06)

A fence—a fascination. Pride in borders.
And yet your grandpa merely dreamed of making
That pipe-formed ornament, still daily taking
Happiness from a task unstarted. Hoarders

Of sweet oneiric territory-orders,
Marking the placement of a self and staking
Invested dream-time in imagined slaking
Of thirsty want of rootedness, recorders

Of courtyard boundaries—they can afford
Reveries of a fence that they will make.
It is a kind of compensation-prize

Replacement for an unreceived reward:
Easy acceptance for mere friendship's sake—
Not to feel alien under others' eyes.

And here are more thoughts on a Romanian legacy, this
time from my own experience:

Romanian-style *Doina*
(1/10/07)

Rumania would perduring favor lend
When, playing on the violin a *doina*,

Joying as if we were about to join a
Wild klezmer caravan, I led my friend,

Who plays piano and accordion:
We flew—swirled up, spun 'round, and swept away
By chords that shifted in unflagging play
Of cloud and sunburst. Thus, when we were done,

The deep impression had been deeply shared,
As of an ancient world of music mages,
Where melody, as in the Middle Ages,

Unbound by any bar-line, gloomed and flared,
Cried in D minor, in G major gleamed:
Románi, shouting, smiled. Or grieved. And dreamed...

One of the best of my Romanian musical adventures:

Taraf de Haidouks: Romani Romania on CD
for Hannah Zacks and Andrei Guruianu
(12/26/07)

Swaying and winding, wavering, it weaves
A partly *ponticello* stroke that near the bridge
Will thin the violinning. Then, a midge
Whirling will flute above the lightest of the leaves.

The Dorian or D-start white key scale
Augmented seconds alter, F and then G sharp.
Soft thrumming will accompany a wail
On mandolin, guitar, a címbalom, a harp.

The major-y to minor-ish will shift.
A vagary, velleity—slow-motion trill
In a prolonged soliloquy to fill
A languor and an anguish with a lilt, a lift.

A rasp, as of a waspy washing board,
Offered a choler-commentary on a mood
    A wayward moaner had imbued
With random-rhythmic rankling anger loud-outpoured.

23. Bartók. I've loved his music for decades. When a senior in high school, I had piano lessons for a year (with a summer at each end) from Wilhelmina Creel Driver in Bloomington IN. I got them for free in return for a set of yellow-jacket immunizing shots Mrs. Driver received from my mother, who was a practicing physician (female doctors being a rarity in 1950s Hoosierland, I'm proud of my mother's pioneering courage). Mrs. Driver had studied piano for some time with Bartók himself; she had simply gone to Hungary, showed up at his home, and asked for lessons! Bartók's black and white photo portrait was on the wall next to the piano. I learned amazingly lovely simple but modally innovative tunes from *Mikrokosmos.* I liked the Hungarian composer's writing so much that I was surprised to be somewhat unimpressed by the seemingly willful discords in a concerto of his that I heard—I had never wanted to have *any* reservations about Bartók. But reading notes by a critic on the record liner, I learned to cope with my mixed reaction:

Bartók, Second Piano Concerto
(7/29/07)

Willful soliloquy—a moody "teen"
(New meaning—"adolescent"; older—"grief"),
Lone, weary wandering with no relief—
Then sudden cannon fire that would careen

Percussive comets into vapid splutter.
I wasn't eager to be too severe...
From childhood, he had often charmed my ear.
But I indulged a grumpy mental mutter.

Notes Boris Gontarev, who's holding court:
"Agglomerated," "polymodal" chords—
Their "ostentatious disssonance" affords

A vaunting, a display, with minimal
Efforts at hinted folktunes. Comment full
Of admirable candor—soul support!

The *Bagatelles* brought back pleasantly my *Mikrokosmos* time:

In every bagatelle of the Bartók set
(5/31/17)

In every bagatelle of the Bartók set
We're taught the deep effect of the finger-touch
     As in a calm Cathayan painting
    Stroke of the brush is a feeling-token.

Though *Microcosm* tunes in the children's book
Developed each a feeling, we here will find
     An episode, with alteration:
    Delicate subtlety, then an outbreak.

The suddenness of change, and rubato—too,
With storm-and-waning—"moody" would be the term
     I'd pick, as when in teenage troubles
    Meaning will swing between all and nothing.

And here's my most heartfelt tribute—recalling an ecstatic time as violin pupil—to the great master:

Béla Bartók, double delight revealing
(5/22/17)

Béla Bartók, double delight revealing,
Granted to my youth-mind a twofold insight.

I, a seventh grader, my birthday present
> Looked at and marveled:

Forty-four Duets. In the second volume
One selection started in six-eight timing;
Two bars done—then quickly a five-eight followed;
> Three-four, the next one.

When the piece I played with my teacher later,
How amazing: natural, every measure,
Though our alterations in timing differed!
> How could it happen?

Tones combined were also a bit peculiar:
I would play F natural and my teacher
Sounded loud F sharp at the selfsame moment.
> Peppery, spicy!

Tempos crazed, and yet in coordination—
Wild the crisis-liking diminished seconds—
All so perfect, beautiful, strange—I'm crying,
> Now, as I tell it.

24. Milhaud. Here is a love song I wrote about Milhaud's
love songs:

Savoir Vivre
(5/19/06)

A warm, a moving light on harbor water—
Milhaud, *La cheminée du roi René*—
Parading pigeon, afternoon café—
Jeanne de Laval, beloved, queenly daughter

Of old Provence—that hearth of arts *Le Coeur*
(The knightly heart alive) *d'amours espris*—

Off on a quest for Dame Doulce-Mercý
Where Shame, Denial, Fear are holding her—

I see you at a table in Marseilles,
Musing the tuneful woodwind harmonies
In quaint-archaic sequence. It will please
A monarch-melodist, a dulcet lay.

A suite—of chivalry a heartfelt dream
Seen by the flow and sparkle of a stream.

25. Piazzolla. I had been utterly unfamiliar, I'm embarrassed to admit, with the work of this much-loved composer—but I savor the bandoleón especially because I've long loved playing fiddle in ensembles with concertina. The instrument often comes to mind when I'm thinking of the joys I've had as folk musician:

An e-mail friend informed me that although
for Matthew Corrigan
(3/6/18)

An e-mail friend informed me that although
It mightn't be quite safe to dare the snow,
He'd host the Tuesday music-time tonight
Should valor with discretion wisely go.

A fine group portrait, too, he sent to show
Five sailors merry, sharing their delight:
Flute, fiddle, banjo, concertina, bright
And tinkling triangle—more happy sight

On shipboard never—"Yes, you want to say,
But what might link the picture to Millay?"
I'll get to that—I've three more lines, okay?

Coordinated tones in wholesome glee
Can charm in varied-timbred harmony:
Cecilia's angel-strayers, they and she.

26. Schumann. The protean Robert Schumann wrote
fugues on the name of BACH. I'll explain what that means:

A Romanticist Bach we have heard from Glenn Gould
on hearing Bachiana: Bach-Transformationen von Moscheles,
Schumann, Reinecke (SWR recording by Duo d'Accord)
(7/10/18)

A Romanticist Bach we have heard from Glenn Gould:
'Twas a kind where the *daimon* the timings had ruled.
And the training we gained will advantage you here—
Schumann, Moscheles, Reinecke's work to endear.

When the Germans refer to the musical keys,
B converts into H; and B flat, if you please,
In the system Teutonic is simply a B.
If you keep this in mind you will readily see

'Twas a practical task for six fugues to be writ
Based on B-A-C-H. 'Tis a tune that is fit,
In chromatic potential, for Schumann to use
When with passion original fugues he'd infuse.

Twelve of Moscheles' Preludes the Duo d'Accord,
Two piano grandmasters, have chosen—and more
Of invention and energy few will require
To the heights of Romantic Baroque who aspire.

When Carl Reinecke varied the Bach Sarabande
He of tunes quite chromatic proved equally fond,
So the Bachian theme in a work of great worth
Will have hastened away from the place of its birth.

Now here is the wizard Schumann transforming Paganini:

Seeking the deep while avoiding the shallow— attractive idea?
(11/12/18)

Die Antwort der Sängerin

Freundin, was ist Gesang? "Gesang ist, wenn du nur hörest,
  Ernst wirst oder weinst, oder dich inniger freust.
Arien all' der Bravur sind nur Schulübungen, die man
  Hält, zu lernen des Tons Bildungen für den Gesang."
Also ist nicht Gesang die Bravura? "Sie sammelte schöne
  Farben in Massen mit Kunst; aber hat sie gemalt?"
    —Friedrich Gottlieb Klopstock

Reply of the Singer

Lady, pray tell, What is song? "You will know it as soon as
  you hear it:
  Grave you become, or you cry, or you may inward
  rejoice.
Airs that are made for bravura are homework for school—it
  will teach you
  How to form tones you can use later when truly you
  sing."
Isn't bravura true song? "No, it merely collected some lovely
  Colors in masses with art. Question: does that mean to
  paint?"

Seeking the deep while avoiding the shallow—attractive
  idea?
  Tricky, I find it, to tell what in each group may belong...
Handel an aria carefully shaped so the features would be a
  Vehicle meant for a "star," pleasing the crowd with the
  song.

Once I had vaguely supposed, being earnest and yet rather
    callow,
    Writing for "flashy" effect, acrobat-athlete to aid,
Meant Paganini and Liszt would be lesser, or lessened, or
    shallow—
    Error I now would renounce! Great Robert Schumann
    had made—

So I'd be learning—from each Paganini caprice a new version
    Clara his sister could play—pianist, she, and the best.
Rivalry, sweet competition—they're part of our total
    immersion
    Deep in the glories of art—*challenge*! and *passing the
    test*!

Schumann the lyric symphonist made an indelible
impression on me when he wrote the tonal equivalent of an
Arabian *qasidah*, an elegy for a maiden seen at a now vanished
campsite in the desert:

Schumann Echoes: Elegy in Bedouin Style
a terza rima sonnet for Tarek Shamma
(2/16/06)

Laßt mich weinen, umschränkt von Nacht. —Goethe

A theme (third movement, fourth great symphony),
A simple wistful ruminative plaint—
Though placid, plangent—made the past, for me,

Come back, the time when I would love to paint
A desert camp, a devastated place,
Where one swift glance that might persuade a saint

Lanced me with dark-bright eyes. It turned—that face—
Enswathed in languid warmth by her endued...
How, later, might I bear the lack of trace

Of tent or path? She couldn't be pursued.
Immense the emptiness the dune displayed.
However much I otherwise had rued

That vanishment, my spirit, grateful, prayed
In firmest faith. Her eye fire cannot fade.

And here is the Schumann I love most, the one I came to know by playing, with friend Asher Raboy, the composer's D Minor Violin and Piano sonata:

Robert Schumann
on a charcoal sketch of him by Aubrey Schwartz
(3/4/06)

The eyes unfocused? Rather, I would say,
They center on two separated things.
The foxhunt—French-horn herald-headed—brings
In train the *lieder*-heaven, yet the way

From one motif-mood to another? Not
Controlled, not known. Piano, violin,
Back to the hunt (D minor), warming in
Pursuant fervor, turn to cordial thought:

A fragmentary grand chorale—in four—
Is blent with chase in climax. What is next?
A pizzicato love plaint! Cute! Perplexed?
Become twi-minded, Schumann-pupil! For

He knew he had twin souls within one man.
They're named "Eusebius" and "Florestan."

I want also to pay homage here to Debussy, who arranged the six études of Schumann for two pianos. The French composer's trio sonata for flute, viola, and harp was the single

work that first enabled me to feel, to comprehend, the perfection
of his craft:

Claude Debussy
on a charcoal sketch of him by Aubrey Schwartz
(3/2/06)

I view him puzzled by a Balinese
Group-gamelan—quick-hammered blocks of wood.
(A scale of whole tone intervals? *I* could
Do that...) Recall a study—just black keys:

"The Girl with Flaxen Hair." I loved the three
Contrasting instrumental timbre hues—
Flute, harp, viola trio—where we lose
No trait of individuality:

They're each a different kind of animal—
Deer, flutterby, and bird—'mid flow'ring plants:
A quirky dialogue becomes a dance.
The lyric dreams of Debussy are full

Of seeming-random rendezvous of these
Experimental, questing melodies.

27. Sarasate. Though I've never written about this wonder-
working violinist-composer, I do love the Spanish folk tradition
he comes from:

Song arising to the mouth
my thoughts on the first line of a Spanish folk song:
"Cantar que sube a la boca"
(12/26/17)

"Song arising to the mouth
Is a honey-drop that comes
From an overbrimmng heart."

Wind-breath wafting from the south
Brings to you the halidoms
Of a man's devoted art.

Soul a melody begot
Pollinated by the bee
That on field of beauty fed.

Dearest maiden, take the thought
That for you melodiously
Love to sweet expression led.

Bloom unfolds to drink the air
That on summer wind arose
And to you, my life, is borne.

Darling of my hope, most fair,
May the tune that overflows
Hearten you this heaven-morn.

28. Enescu. One of the most profound visionaries (clairaudients?) of the 20th century, Enescu merits far more attention than he has gained. The orchestral suites are magnificent. The first line of my poem refers to the self-prompting of Renaissance poet Sir Philip Sidney in the final line of sonnet 1 from *Astrophel and Stella*: "...look in thy heart and write."

29. Dohnányi. When I wrote about him earlier, I was only just beginning to appreciate his work (see also **76. Martinů**):

Recital: Mark Rudoff and Sandra Joy
cello and piano works with variations
(10/14/10)

The *Magic Flute* caprice of Beethoven? No hint,
Though elegant and tasteful, of the titan-fight

To come, with…
> Kabalevsky? Thought that he was "light"!
(Those things on violin for children…) Fingerprint,

Not theme, was given for the variation suite:
A three-note series of a half-step, then a whole.
Seems major—yet it lent the piece a minor soul.
The second movement was a retrospection feat

As if a boy'd been told he ought to write a waltz
In soft Tchaikovsky mode: he, hesitating, halts,
Inserting, here and there, a shiver, or a smirk.

Dohnányi—canorous and ample Brahms-y work.
I sadly haven't time to analyze it well.
Then Martinů's Rossini cast a comic spell!

My violin teacher at the Indiana University School of Music in the academic year 1958–1959, who had been for 20 years the head of the Budapest Academy of Music, was not only a friend of, but musical collaborator with Dohnányi, as well as with Bartók. At the former's home in Tallahassee Zathureczky played with him a taped concert issued on CD; and with the latter he played a concert at the hall of the Korona Hotel in Nyíregyháza on January 10, 1934 (Wikipedia). Here is my tribute:

My Teacher, Ede Zathureczky (1903–1959)
to his treasured memory
(1/10/06)

Dohnányi, Bartók had he known.
He smoked. While he would teach me, ash
Fell on my fiddle. That alone
Was risky. But on his? A rash
Habit, in fact his hand would shake

Not only for vibrato's sake.
A passionate and kindly man,
He taught me how the player can
Give breath to anything he plays:
A cat tail moving, cracking whip—
They're each a metaphoric tip
For limber, independent ways
Three levers in the arm, the hand
At varied speeds are moving and—

Breathe! For the rising and the fall
From shoulder to the fingers will
Create *bel canto*. That is all
We most can want. The singer still
May in my lifted arm respire,
As he advised, and rarely tire.
Vivaldi, Mozart, Beethoven…
He said, on one occasion when
I wasn't playing properly,
"What happened? Are you tired today?
Maybe you fell in love? You play
Strangely." How well he spoke to me!
I was fifteen. That was the year
He died. No teacher, friend, more dear.

I should explain a little more fully what Prof. Zathureczky taught me. He said that the changing of the bow, the movement of the three independent levers it required, was the central part of violin playing, enabling the musician to "breathe" with the bow. The levers—upper arm, forearm, and hand—had different lengths and each of them moved on its own midpoint or "fulcrum," simultaneously with the others, but always at their own separate speeds. This was so crucial that after my first lesson Prof. Zathureczky told me not to touch the violin for a week but rather to devote all my practice time to making the motions of the independently moving

simultaneous levers while miming the act of changing the
bow—not holding the bow but imagining it—and observing
your miming in a mirror. You were to think of objects moving
in slow motion; cat's tail, a whip, a blade of long grass in the
wind were helpful images-in-motion:

Violin Lesson in the Manner of Ede Zathureczky
(5/31/11)

Thomas Hardy would dance when his father would play
On the fiddle and so, reproducing the tune
With his body, could make in a lyrical way
A translation in space of the musical rune.

Now the trees of the wood, when they sigh in the wind
With their branches, each ramification, asway,
Are the dancers, poetic, of breath violinned,
That the rising, subsiding of heart will portray.

For the change of the bow to be supple indeed
Will require that the upper arm, lower arm, hand
Be construed as the levers they are, and command,
Every one independent, a separate speed.

On their several fulcrums, the three will repeat
At their differing tempos the free-breathing heart,
The subsiding and rising in seesawing art
That are shaping the phrasing and making it sweet.

Arm extended, the bow-changing motion you make
Gentle movement of cat-tail in air will recall,
Flicking whip in slow motion or, softest of all,
Inclination of reeds in the breeze near a lake.

You can see that the fiddler is doing a dance
That, embodying feelings of breathing, will go

More than half of the way to a lyric and so
Putting feet into motion, the soul will enhance.

30. Khatchaturian. The parenthetical second quatrain might make you wonder, Why include this? I grabbed the chance to show the ease of transitions between life and art. Such casual stunts and whimsy are meant to counteract any predisposition against the intricate formal shapings I always love the most. Friendly competitors in art-prowess want to show the cheering crowd "how easy it is."

31. Rossi. Preparing a Salomone Rossi hymn (set to Hebrew lyrics by this Venetian Renaissance composer) as a tenor in the Binghamton University-Community Chorus conducted by William Culverhouse, I was moved to the following *Herzensergießung*:

Alcaics for Energy
roused by Rossi, "Odecha Ki Anitani"
(9/12/17)

Let's grant I have a task—even two or three—
But need to keep the sense that I yet am free:
        By prefacing or interspersing
    Writings I've chosen, in prose or versing,

I feel the whoosh of Liberty Victor surge!
From convict-mood will never delight emerge:
        Before the breaker, stand in welcome,
    Bravely alert, whether heav'n or hell come.

Awake, alive, this day that the Lord has made,
I'll cry Give Praise! till finally down I'm laid.
        Hymn, elevate my obligation,
    Bidding it sing with a soul-elation.

Be rival! Temerarious, teach aright
Your younger brother: lift to a higher light

The torch that speeds your bridegroom-racing,
Juiced with the hues that the trees are gracing!

What some had rubble deemed, a rejected stone
With scorn to distant field by the builders thrown,
Behold reclaimed by those enshrining
What the divine had been long divining.

Unless the house be raised to the height of psalm
In vain the makers labor. A strength in calm
Will rouse from underground the fountain
Centuries buried beneath their mountain!

32. Bach or Not Bach. This poem, based on a little experiment in listening, barely begins to hint at the treasure-legacy of J. S. Bach, my favorite of all composers I have ever heard. Here's a fuller tribute:

How the Blessings of Bach May be Daily Multiplied for the Benefit of All Creatures
(7/9/07)

How could a violinist ever have more fun?
Last week I played sonata-trios one through four
By J. S. Bach, composed for organ, then redone
To suit two violins with keyboard (cello). More

Delight arrived today: sonatas five and six—
Continuo and violin. The colors—new.
And textures. And sensations. And ideas, too.
Alive's each line of counterpoint when we unmix

All blurry blending muddying the single way
A soul need travel, unpredictable, distinct.
Know each one by itself. Then you may know them linked.

The wayward, strange, extravagating modes of play
Of minds that wander here and seem to go astray
Meet yonder. "It is good," the Maker said—and winked.

Let's try even harder for adequate homage:

Thoughts on a Bach Cantata Strophe
(1/27/10)

Des Höchsten Gegenwart allein
Kann unsrer Freuden Ursprung sein.
Vergeh Du, Welt, mit Deiner Pracht,
Denn Gott hat was uns glücklich macht.

"The presence of the Highest can
Alone be source of joy to man.
Grand world in glory, vanish! We
By God are giv'n felicity."

The setting by the master may
In triple time our strife allay;
Then let the mind in heaven dance
And light within the laughing glance.

The world if distant will return:
The fires are one that nightly burn
In us, and in the farther star,
With yearnings that eternal are.

The earth itself that inly shakes
And molten ore a-borning makes
To bolt and roar with solar force
Will indicate our stellar course.

I praise the six-wing'd angel-flame
Seraphic as the dance-acclaim

That bounds when mountain, shouting, leaps,
For deepest ground no secret keeps.

My hymn or plaint, the wind I breathe
Are kin to storms that wailing seethe:
May even tears their heat release
From searing war to soaring peace.

The heart to courage gave its name,
And energy hard birth might claim
In work, the ergonomic law
That isn't tame but strong and raw.

The worthy time when work is done
Will ardent rise from carmine sun
And urge the rhyme of surging blood
In thudding might with tidal flood.

Let granted labor stay the test,
That I with pray'r-expanded breast
Arising life attain whereby
Surrender may the mind ensky.

    I can't keep from adding a couple of briefer tributes:

Johann Sebastian Bach
on a charcoal sketch of him by Aubrey Schwartz
(3/4/06)

The richest feeling is the deepest thought.
Behold the great and godlike paradox
Letting us call Johann Sebastian Bach's
Work a transcendence of the human lot.

An obbligato, aria, chorale
He will combine; the perfect shape of each

Enhancing all the other forms will reach
Ear, mind, heart, spirit. In a pastorale

The "Joy of Man's Desiring" he achieved.
"Art of the Fugue," a solar system of
Planet-motifs revolving, shows the love
A god has for a world. I have believed

That Brandenburg Concerto Number Five
Will always make me glad I am alive.

Bach
(9/8/13)

Glad thought there came to me when young:
To hear a Bach cantata sung
In glory on the radio
Must largen, strengthen, heart and lung

As, feeling Eden-branches grow
In scope to greet the Ah and O,
We're drawn as well by heaven-kiss
Twined hymns to comprehend, and know

(Blest "Endlich wird mein Joch..."!) the bliss
That reigns when, at the height of this,
The brain, the soul no more can try
To compass multiples. Abyss—

More sought than feared—is little death
From which in slow-recovered breath,
When mind-spent and emotion-wrung,
We go where Spirit summoneth.

Permit, I entreat, a supplementary laudation:

Doch weichet, ihr tollen, vergeblichen Sorgen!
for Katharina Mommsen
(5/1/18)

Doch weichet, ihr tollen, vergeblichen Sorgen!
   Mich rufet mein Jesus, wer sollte nicht gehn?...
Erscheinet mir, seliger, fröhlicher Morgen,
   Verkläret und herrlich vor Jesu zu stehn.

[Be banished and vanish, O maddening sorrow!
   My Jesus—He calls me—I'll gladly depart.
Appear to me—festive and blesséd—dear Morrow—
   Transfigured in vision—flee Christward, my heart!]

How many—unnumbered!—the times I have listened:
   The voice and the flute, so enamored, entwined...
The eyes, rapt in happiness—crying, they glistened
   At air, obbligato—they're heaven-combined!

I heard it performed on the radio—rarely...
   'Twould let me foretell: once or twice, every year
The time would arrive when—preparédly, yarely—
   The number—belovéd—I'd gratefully hear.

Cantatas befriended me: starting age twenty,
   I'd follow the text I'd to memory lend.
Unendingly apt, variations aplenty
   Each air to complexity vast would extend.

It often occurred to me: Beethoven's human,
   And manlike the passionate realm he portrays—
But Bach from the viewpoint of God, of the Numen,
   Inhabits the world he'll pervadingly praise.

There's no other man that has trod on this planet
   So kindred in wandering mode to my soul.

The Art of the Fugue—Isaac Newton might scan it
    And grasp of each note the harmonious role.

Bach's *Musical Offering,* containing a trio sonata that I played in high school with friends Kyril Magg on flute and Daniel Rothmuller on double bass (yes, that's right!), deepened my feeling for what music could do:

Homage to Bach: Ovidian Distich Sonnet
(2/5/06)

Now that I'm into my sixties, a life-writing whim-drive
        arises:
    Think of a moment that sowed light in awakening days:
Magianly musical. One in particular brightly comprises
        What from a fire-seed may grow, branching in ramified
        praise.

Wholly engrossed in the college's music-tape archive
        recording,
    I, yet in high school, intent fully on hearing each part,
Voices, alone and together, polyphony-rapture affording,
        Avidly trying to find what was alluring my heart—

Bach, *Musikalisches Opfer,* the trio sonata, I wanted
    Truly, completely, to hear, *hear* every note in the score.
Movement? The second, *Allegro,* arrestingly jaunty, had
        haunted
    Me and my friends who had played, often, the work, but
        the more,

Now, that I willed that my brain might contain what the
        Master had written,
Lord! all the fainter I felt—love!—overpowered—and smitten!

One day, utterly overcome, I even dared to write the following:

Beethoven and Bach
(6/15/11)

There is a time in Beethoven's quartet
When quick arpeggiated sudden dance
With swaying body, waving hair, and some-
thing fiery and defiant in the eyes

Will make the violin example set
Of how the sanity of shaman-glance
Appeared a mad attack and yet must come
To one who'll hallelu when heart is wise.

To him, the prophet, God had shown His face.
But one I know that, deeper yet, His mind
Had shared and more than merely human place

Attaining, heard in movement intertwined
Of atom, planet, galaxy, and man
The soul of Bible-word and Alcoran.

I have listened to all the cantatas of Bach, which because
of modern technology may be bought from Brilliant CDs in a
single box that can be dandled on the lap. Here's an excited
reply:

Bach Cantata: Composite Impression

A melissal melisma will lissomely twist
    And a singer be blissfully kissed,
For the horn and the shawm, bringing storm and then calm,
    To the spirit are balsam and balm.

When the trumpet and drum told the dragon had come
    That his blight to the light might succumb,
While the blind and benighted whose pride had defied,
    As the cellos tell, fell by the side,

Then the prayer for peace lent a saving release
    To the seeker upon the decease
Of the enemy, sin, that in envy won't win
    With his venom that withers within.

Musing flutes in a unison tunefully croon
    While the oboes will moan. The bassoon,
To a tympani boom, offers laughter some room,
    Counteracting satanical gloom.

For when energy entered the center of men
    And of women to send out again
From the heat of the heart, through the ardor of art,
    Blazing rays to the farthermost part,

It was so that we'd grow, and could momently know,
    What slow glowing a flow would bestow.
Be the sweetness of freedom astream through the trees,
    Vatic, avid beatitude-breeze.

In a soft-swelling phrasing, upwelling of praise,
    Who would anthem the grandeur of days
Will engender a genesis never to end—
    Angel errand and messenger friend.

I can never voice adequate thanks to Bruce Borton and the Binghamton University-Community Chorus he conducted, for offering me the chance to sing tenor in Bach's *B Minor Mass*. One day I visited an aquarium, then rehearsed the *Mass* in the evening:

Aquarium and Choir Practice
(9/23/07)

Sea creatures marching hard on miles-down mire!
A pounding swishing sound, a hiss and beat,

Enframed—blue gel, and ultra wave, and wire—
That amplify the blood rush in my feet.

Brave-raying circulation loud and fleet
And proud in playing, ground-bass to the choir
Of unheard companies of movers, wheat
And wine to feed and heat a neural fire—

Bright mindward climb, enskying of desire:
Tonight I sing *B Minor Mass*, more sweet
Accentuating of the pow'r, entire
And hale, who guess marine beasts' wish to meet

More soundings in the deep of drum and stream,
Red blood, blue air, white ganglion, green dream.

    I'm tempted to say Bach ennobles everyone with whom he associates. A case in point:

Johann Ernst von Sachsen-Weimar and J. S. Bach
(7/10/07)

Johann Ernst von Sachsen-Weimar. Who was he?
Well—we'd never know if Bach had not decided
Violin concertos ought to be provided
(Good ones, anyway) with keyboard versions we

Know today transcribed. We hear them gratefully.
Music history would slyly have elided
One I'll bet you knew as little of as Í did.
Bach has lent him life, presented him to me.

Two concertos were Vivaldi-like. The three
Others equaled them. Sequential phrases glided
By with easy adolescent energy.

Fame was playing dice. But when she tossed the die, did
Anyone predict that Johann Ernst would be
One with whom the random hand of chance had sided?

I'd also like to introduce a lyric that my teacher Katharina
Mommsen of Stanford University has discovered was written
by Johann Wolfgang von Goethe apropos of a Bach performance
and, though untitled, is dedicated to Bach. I'll translate the
lyric ("Laß mich hören...") and offer a brief "comment":

Let me hear, and let me feel [Goethe's Tribute to Bach]

Let me hear, and let me feel,
How the sound speaks to the heart.
In these cooler days, appeal
Warmth and light in spendthrift art.

Ready empathy assuring
In a major work new-born,
What is primal and enduring
Fears no criticaster scorn.

What arises ever-living,
Kindred to the spirit-choir,
Uncompelled and freely giving
Builds a world to our desire.

The disciple from the Master
Laudable advantage gains.
For the mind will ripen faster
Moved by what that Soul attains.

Comment on Goethe's Tribute to Bach

You have said it, *lieber* Goethe.
Bach, to me, was such a man,

An enfolding *Morgenroethe*
Showing what the spirit can—

Gladly warmth and light expending
As a Danaë to them
That would grow and glow, extending
An Olympic anadem.

By the love that such a spirit
Lends to every heart on earth
Godliness we know, and near it
In a golden-grown rebirth.

Teurer Bach, who are an ocean
Ev'n as Beethoven had claimed,
You have set the soul in motion
And divine are rightly named.

Here, finally, is a little postscript, just for fun:

Treadmill Cardio Cantata
(3/11/07)

Schleuß des Janustempels Türen! Close
Gates of two-way facing, discord, strife.
Open heart and voice, declare for life!
Comes the third Augustus, he that rose

From Elector, now is Polish King.
Danube, Vistula, two rivers more
Clap their hands while flute and oboe soar;
Glides the violin, encouraging,

Crisped and curled, the wavelets to adorn
Might and majesty with arabesque
Ornament, baroquely humoresque,

Riding tides of trumpet, drum, and horn.
Amply laud the lord of Saxony!
Bach has made his birthday bright for me.

33. Byrd. It seems logical to juxtapose Byrd and Bach,
as I do here:

Reckless, turbulent spree William Byrd can set free
(10/19/18)

Reckless, turbulent spree William Byrd can set free
    In the two-note themed "Bells." You'll agree,
When you hear what that harpsichord keyboard can do,
    'Tis predicting the storm coming through

In the improvisation of Brandenburg Five,
    Where the hands with temerity strive
To evade all constraint, so that Bach may present
    What the life of a striver has meant.

To each quick French coranto in contrast we dance,
    And with bounce could the rhythm enhance
In "Lord Willobies Welcome" the words that would then
    Joy the ear when remembered again.

Seven discs! We can, favored by miracle, hear
    What delighted Elizabeth's ear,
And the song-variations are Byrd at his best—
    When he heard dear Cecilia blest.

Here is a time-travel experience with this English composer
and a couple of his Italian contemporaries:

Canadian Brass
(7/21/07)

They're playing Gabrieli, Monteverdi, Byrd
And bringing back the time of childhood when I'd go

Across the street—eight-thirty, homework done—and so
Entitled to a free recital. Hymns I heard—

By heaven's will—one blessed night! A twinned brass choir.
One group on stage, another in the balcony,
Above my head their dialogue they played—to me
Immersion in those tones meant bright blue mind afire.

Piazza di San Marco. Gabrieli near.
For in the vaulted halls of the cathedral, clear
The sounds ring out! remembered now, imagined here.

Out in the square I diarized and heard the band
Of well-skilled minstrel-men. Three hours my writing hand
Moved to the drift of tunes in Gabrieli-land.

34. Mendelssohn. His String Symphonies are a tonic for
the making-drive. Some have claimed that Mendelssohn was
in a way even more prodigious at the beginning than Mozart
had been, since when the two boys' compositions done at the
same age are compared, those of Mendelssohn prove better
and more mature.

Wunderkind
(6/8/06)

String Symphony. Think limpidly. Unproud,
A prayer outburst from behind a cloud.
A thirteen-year-old boy. A flower bowed.
A man is born. A might poured forth, aloud.

It is the ninth one that the youth has made.
Reflect upon the favorite portrayed:
Alight, in aural rainbow-robe arrayed,
Sky-Joseph, color-waving unallayed.

288 ♫ *Martin Bidney*

A miracle, the lyric filled the room.
A bright arising from an opened womb.
Auroral rose, it gleamed away the gloom.
It moistened eyes, the dew upon the bloom.

Musicians, we created were for this,
Young Mendelssohn—bar-mitzvah of our bliss.

The string symphony by 13-year-old Felix Mendelssohn brought to mind the child-voice in his later oratorio *Elijah*, along with an event in my own life when I was 13, the age when the Jewish bar-mitzvah rite is held:

In Mendelssohn's *Elijah* we find (scene five—

In Mendelssohn's *Elijah* we find (scene five—
The center of the nine) that a child is told
Three times, "Go up, and gaze at the heav'n, and say,
                    What do you see there?"

The first two tries no cloudlet on high would yield,
But then—the final triumph—a roaring storm!
The child-tone I to angels' would liken—sweet,
                    Pure, and endearing.

When I became bar mitzvah, I too performed—
To aid the service. First came the blessing-chant,
Then Torah-cantillation, the Kiddush last:
                    Maybe they saved me...

A crisis might have risen: when called to give
My talk to show interpretive skill, I found
I couldn't bring myself to come out with what
                    Wasn't authentic.

My father and the rabbi the lesson planned
That I'd expound: they'd argued it back and forth.

I wrote what they directed but—in the end—
> *Couldn't recite it.*

I thanked the congregation for kindness lent
In giving me a beautiful place to pray
And mark the grand occasion—I meant it all,
> Then I was quiet.

I think I proved my manhood, although my voice
Had not yet changed. And no one a comment made—
Not then or later. Maybe my chanting gave
> Adequate pleasure.

I am deeply enamored of Mendelssohn's *Elijah*, which I sang in Binghamton University/Community Chorus under the direction of Bruce Borton. Here's another poem which that oratorio helped me to conceive:

Love for the One

O Lord, my Creator,
How excellent Thy name is
Amo♪ng the♪ nations:
Thou fillest all the heav'ns with
Thy glo♪-o♪-ry.
A-♪♪♪-men,
A-♪♪♪-men!
> —concluding fugue to Mendelssohn,
> Elijah: An Oratorio

The nightingale and lark are small;
Though condor, eagle tower tall,
They cannot equal those in song,
Nor serve with hymn in heaven-hall.

That pow'r of singer-flight be strong,
To skiey height will wings belong,

But tone let widened breast be lent
By Allah-throne to thrill the throng.

The air is heaven-element,
Yet twinned is melody-intent:
More deep the breath, intense the light,
So flames are from the seraph sent.

Love-honeyed lips of him are bright
Whose heartstring lyre is benedight,
Outpouring to the Lord of all
The sonar gold of lightning-sight.

    Over the years, the early works of the wonder-child continued to have their effect on me:

Intuitive
(8/27/16)

"Each movie customer we see,"
My daughter said in mild surprise,
"Can understand one language." Wise—
Not often thought of—artistry:

"You say a word and it will be
What people understand." Bright eyes—
She taught me more than you'd surmise.
A Mendelssohn string symphony

Made clear: below each tone there lies
A mood-assumed community:
They understand each other. Skies

Reveal the angels wordlessly
Conversing, light-ray-like, so we
Are told by old theology.

An artist friend brought me an unusual but penetrating vision of the composer:

Felix Mendelssohn
on a charcoal sketch of him by Aubrey Schwartz
(3/2/06)

A drypoint made with metal plate where grooves
Were deeply cut presented Mendelssohn
More dark and rougher than was ever done
Before—wild whiskers, windswept hair, it moves

The viewing eye in curves around the space
Ungovernably and capriciously
As the finale in the key of E
Allows the solo violin to race

With prestidigitation to the end
Of rapt concerto in a breathless whirl.
So implications of an airy swirl
Are felt to breathe about the face, and lend

A feeling we are dwelling in the mind
Where humming elfin summer dreams unwind.

I especially want to celebrate the master's piano works:

Mendelssohn Piano Sonatas
(8/8/07)

What do the *West-East Divan* and a Men-
delssohn sonata for piano share?
Playfulness. True, the gravity is there,
But—that refreshing levity! And when

He takes a motive learned from Bach, again
Capriciously he turns into an air

Recitative-like writing. With a flair
For unpredictables he'll fugue it. Then

He'll sing a *Lied* or ballad—very spare
And simple outline. But—the clinamen:
A counter-motive, rumbling low, to dare

Peace to endure! The song-mood, free of care;
Each presto—elvish dancing in a fen;
Maybe a Hebridean hermit-prayer...

    Mendelssohn so embodies the pure, transforming hymn-will of the singing instinct that he rises before me with heliacal warmth:

Then Let Us Rage Before the Reign of Sleep
(4/22/15)

The *Lobgesang* of Mendelssohn to give
To that infinity it issued from
And roaring glorify the halidom
Which cries, *TO BE* and *NEVER CEASE TO LIVE*

Must mean the shout I from the body free—
As if with strong right hand and outstretched arm
To drown the plaguy prose with flood alarm,
To lead the exodus to poetry,

To make the noun a seven-branchéd verb—
Unfearing of the sneer-attack acerb,
To ford the Jordan, with menorah come

To where the critic-word is stricken dumb,
To sing with timbrel, psalm with barbiton
The solar horses of the force of dawn.

35. Bernstein. In high school I played violin in the overture to *Candide*. As tenor in Binghamton University-Community Chorus conducted by Bruce Borton I twice performed *Chichester Psalms*. Most recently a year ago I saw, and was revived by, *West-Side Story* at Glimmerglass Opera in Cooperstown NY. I brought the latter two works together in a very early poem:

Choir Concert
for Bruce Borton, conductor of the Binghamton
University-Community Chorus
(12/24/05)

Storm-shaken forest, wind harp art-enlarged,
Merged in the Mendelssohn *Walpurgisnacht,*
We feel a Druid glory, *Geistesmacht.*
Now, in Moussorgsky, "Coronation," charged

With open chords of lordly liturgy,
We throng the cloud-cathedral of the tsars.
The longing of the grieving seeker jars
The godly calm with atonality—

Then, restful penance—"Prayers of Kierkegaard"
Fraught with the fight of Barber's hope and qualms.
Then, "West Side" chords in Chichester—the "Psalms"!—
A reconciliation rare and hard.

Beethoven, fire-drunk, lit the holy spark.
Prayer-breath. Quietude. The height is dark.

36. Kirchner and **37. Gershwin.** The jazz-inflected numbers helped prepare me for the Jazz Symphony of **81 Antheil.**

38. Lawes. This selection and **65. Boyce** gave me a sense of major happenings in British music between **89 Handel** and **100 Purcell.**

39. Verdi. The performances of *La Traviata* and *Showboat* (see **50 Kern and Hammerstein**) at Glimmerglass Opera this past summer reminded me how crucial pervasive melodic beauty, with deeply memorable songs, had been to my enjoyment of operas and musicals.

40. Kodály. If we begin the composition with a sneeze, critics agree, one should take the rogue's autobiographical presentation with more than a handful of salt. Sneezes are evidently pejoratives; I'm thinking of the colloquial English phrase "nothing to sneeze at," that is, "nothing to slight or belittle." Other data on sarcasm and sneezing? I find this in a Catullus poem—which I'll translate:

While Septimius held his lover Acme
tr. MB with comment
Catullus 45
(10/18/17)

While Septimius held his lover Acme
Close to heart he declared: "If with abandon
I no longer can love, and prove unready
For a constant devotion though our lifetimes,
Then—as often as people perish lonesome
'Mid the Lybian heat, the searing swelter
Felt in India—then will I be going
Bold, undaunted, to meet the blue-eyed lion."
Love, approval to show, was sneezing leftward
As it rightward had sneezed before, in answer.

Acme, bending her head in sign of welcome,
Eyes—infatuate—of her lover kissing—
Wine-red lips, a delight for him she favored—
Said, Septimius, life of mine, so be it.
Servants may we remain of one great master,
Letting grander and keener passion kindle,
Burning soft in the marrow of your dear one."

Love, approval to show, was sneezing leftward
As it rightward had sneezed before, in answer.

Having so with a perfect omen started,
Thus they love and are loved in dulcet union,
Poor Septimius, lucky man, attached to
Acme—Syria, Britain both excelling.
As for Acme, she finds her every pleasure
In Septimius only, her beloved.
Who a happier couple could imagine?
Who a passion conceive, a love more blessèd?

Shall we seek for an answer? 'Tis a challenge...
Here's my double reply: "Good health! Gesundheit!"

41. Dowland. And maybe you'll try this, too:

Viol Consort Playing Dowland
(8/16/09)

Bathed in the liquid warmth of welling phrase,
The overlapping interwinding waves,
One with another darkly blending, raise
An arc that, in the center cresting, braves

Immersion in the current as it rides,
Of rolling made that neither roils nor raves,
Yet bounded in its rounding sound by tides
Whereof the young unsundered loving laves—

With running humming of a purling viol
Choir that ancestrally from amber phial
Aromas opened of a soul-surround—

What floats upon the ocean-whirl profound,
Like to a new-fledged bird that resting broods:
Woe of the dolor-torn in mourning moods.

42. Schein. Though only a be-loving imaginer, not a believing one, I love to live in others' worlds and to become those people savoring those worlds.

43. Mahler. The most I had ever dared to write about this titan is a sketch of a sketch:

Gustav Mahler
on a charcoal drawing of him by Aubrey Schwartz
(5/7/06)

A *roman fleuve*, enormous novel-river,
A tonal, many-tomed biography,
Sublime-ironic epic-elegy,
Diary of a moody picture-giver

Are the collected songs and symphonies,
A repertory of remembered themes:
Nature awaking, tranquil valley dreams,
A horrifying storm—and, after these,

A blend of sentimental ländler-schmaltz
With old mock-pompous military band,
Chromatic languid-anxious longing, and
Dead children's heaven-chant, a village waltz—

Porcelain-clear, a lyrical Chinese
Hymn to the earth, to lend the heart some ease.

44. Schütz. Here is another hearing of him:

Heinrich Schütz, *Opus Ultimum*
*motets on the 176 verses of Psalm 119, plus
the hundredth psalm and a German requiem*
(12/6/07)

A hapless passion, man; a symptom, fame.
Yet never think the Deity alone

May rightly have this glory: trumpet-tone
Be judge of those a noble mind would shame!

Because the thirty years of madding war
Had spurned the psalm-life he was writing for,
Eleven double-choir motets he made.
The parts were lost. Now found—so long delayed!

That man of eighty-six (he cannot fail—
Austere the spirit-way through shadowed vale!)
Re-breathes a warm soliloquy of peace.

Each minor clause will close in major chord,
A sign of high defiance in the Lord.
The task enframes the days till last release.

45. Villa Lobos. Life blends with art: the memory of Segovia playing overpowered even the spirit-scope of the Villa Lobos piece—not defeating it in any way but letting the flower fragrance widen into a more spacious reverie.

46. Biber. With the aid of a pianist friend, I once played a Biber rosary sonata in a little house-concert to which I was invited. Thrilled to have mastered the scordatura, I was filled with the expressive power of the invention. The complexity of Biber's endeavor is hard to overstate. Every scordatura piece needs to be printed in two versions: one to indicate what the tones are, and the other to show the performing violinist what the score would look like if one's fingers were in their usual positions in regular tuning. The production of the two versions is such a subtle mental trick that the edition I played from had a number of errors; they're likely inevitable.

47. Janáček. For a strong contrast in mood and genre, try *The Cunning Little Vixen*. I saw a production of it at Glimmerglass Opera—no finer version is imaginable.

We are glad for the badger, the vixen and fox
(7/9/18)

We are glad for the badger, the vixen and fox
And the hens and the rooster when magic unlocks
The capacity hid that their voices reveal—
While the frog and mosquito and dragonfly spiel

Are by themes recognizable, chanter-assigned:
The composer the soul of the life has divined
That the forest will animate after we're gone
And the cycle of death and of life carry on.

Never costume designer was more to be praised
Than the ones who the spirit of woodland have raised
To a height with a child-ingenuity pure
That continuing dancer-delight would assure.

Leoš Janáček, even more "cunning" than she—
Singing vixen—whose life you have chronicled! We
Such an opera never had dreamed to perceive:
In your sylvan fulfilment our hymn-hearts believe.

A few years earlier, also at Glimmerglass, I saw another
opera by this many-dimensioned creator. I'll sing of the story
first, then of the music.

Janáček's *Jenůfa:* The Story
(8/1/06)

Ungainly long-neck'd maiden plainly taken in,
Flattery aiding, by a flashy ambling lout.
Pregnant. Her wailing mother, flailing arms about,
Waiting the hated scion of a stinging sin,

Hounded by Fury, learned remorse when, driven on

Ever more horridly, with ailing, addled brain,
Crazed, she abandoned to perdition what the gain
Of passion-life provided. Now the newborn's down

Deep in the crime-cold winter chill beneath the ice.
"Respectability"—quite "rescued." But the heart,
Omen-alerted, fears—knows! that her evil art
Will out! And yet—the girl's forgiving will suffice

(Bolstered by lifelong love her stepbrother had shown)
Boldly to make a lifeward road—more holy—known.

Janáček's *Jenůfa: The Music*
(8/2/06)

A fragment for
A theme—a shape of two,
Three chosen tones, not many more—
Seedlet of meaning formed in but a few,

Returns, again, again,
Colored and subtly, thoughtfully
Deepened in ardent conversation when,
Bothered, we amplify a thought for clarity.

A swerve. No warning. Key and shape will change.
Found object, harsh or driftwood-sleek, a novel sound.
Odd feeling-curve. No rule. Unmoored. Accumulated
    strange
Arrivals. Altered heart-attention—roused, becalmed, or
    tossed around.

For the brain-waking range of the rhythm, unchaining the
    deadly enigma, the task of the thickening night,
Transvaluing tragedy, banishing rage and a battering
    willfulness, lure of the Fury, has mind-lighting might.

48. Marais. Here's a little more about this lovable composer:

Bach, Rembrandt, Marais
(12/10/07)

The viol consort, "Fretwork," that for me
Performed Bach *contrapuncti,* just tonight,
Brought a forgotten memory to light:
My father's office. There, again, I see

A portrait which was guessed inventively
To picture that philosopher whose might
Of intellect was legend, by the sight
Of olden sculpture livened. My CD

And "Aristotle Contemplating Homer"
Were blent. The brush of Rembrandt, mental roamer,
The low and thoughtful bowing, vocal-toned,

As in the film "Tous les matins du monde"
With music of the Sun King's loved Marais,
Illume the *Summa* that the viols play.

49. Billings. I was introduced to his melodic and contrapuntal gifts when listening to selections on an LP of the 'sixties by the American female vocal ensemble, Western Wind. I am still singing numbers they taught me.

50. Kern and Hammerstein. When I was very young, I one day heard my mother singing "Why Do I Love You?" while she was tidying up the apartment. She almost never sang.

51. Achron takes me back to childhood; I have lived long with this melody.

52. Bulgarian Folk Music returns me to my daughter's

childhood. About the lovable dance rhythms of Bulgarian tradition I wrote this:

In 3 + 3 + 2 we've a way to change
(6/1/17)

In 3 + 3 + 2 we've a way to change
An eight-beat measure: then to the tune we'll add
      Impassioned memorized adornments:
    Fiddle and singer and woodwinds know them.

The man has told a story, and now we'll hear
A woman's heart outpoured in defiant cry:
      The long, long notes in richened valor
    Travel through keys with connective tremblings.

Bulgaria! You've wandered a path distinct
From many other makers of tonal form—
      Conjoining moods of color-contrast
    Loved by the brain for the crazy meters.

The final four-liner of **52. Bulgarian Folk Music** brings to mind a folk song from the Basque tradition that flourishes in Spain and France:

Maitea nun zira - **Voix Basques**
Be at Achiary, Choeur Ama-Lur
(5/22/06)

Chorale, a swelling choir, a yielding lull,
Ripe wheat fields have become a place, a time
Of sweeping wind and quiet—chordal mime
Of rising scythe and grateful rest. They mull,

The singers, tragic lover's plight, while he,
Distracted into madness, makes the tone

A climbing, rasping, harsh coyote moan—
Aggrieved, it falls—a racking, crying plea.

And look!—a woman wails into a shawl
That wraps her face, unwilling to be seen—
Unable, though, to stay unheard, a keen
Cry of entire abandonment by all.

Only a father's hardened heart will keep
Lovers apart, choir-cradled while they weep.

53. Haydn. Here's a supplementary tribute to him (and
to Gabriel Fauré) from a grateful tenor in the Binghamton
University-Community Chorus:

Haydn's *De Angustiis* and Fauré's *Requiem*
for Bruce Borton, our conductor,
with 13 years' worth of gratitude
(3/31/17)

Every psalm that I sing in the hundred-voiced choir
    Joys in calm- or in thunder-desire.
Troubled times in the Haydn, grave care in Fauré,
    Horrid burdens that world-night affray,

Are re-moaned and redeemed: you re-travel the waves
    When a mage with a tone-gift embraves:
All the moods that awake I remake in my heart,
    For Cecilia would sainthood impart

When the poet-composer a testament sung,
    Whom the tides of the ocean kept young.
They are lifeblood within, as you'll readily hear
    When you lift up a shell to the ear.

If a parent should say you are hearing the sea,
    Reply smiling, "The ocean's *in me.*

Through much-amplified echo this object I hold
   Can my ear's tonal blood-flow make bold."

And here's a brief "portrait" in a sonnet to accompany a drawing by my friend, artist Aubrey Schwartz:

Joseph Haydn
on a charcoal sketch of him by Aubrey Schwartz
(5/8/06)

Inventor of the modern string quartet,
"Rococo" he's been called, and yet how far
He traveled from Boucher or Fragonard.
Bouncy Parisian symphonies would get

Their vivid nicknames, "Queen" and "Hen" and "Bear,"
From a suggestive wit, free-spirited.
Heard street-cries of the London vendors led
To echoes in a movement written there.

So often modulations cry "surprise,"
Like the delightful symphony so named.
Pan-European "Papa," though acclaimed,
He kept exploring. Feel the depth of sighs—

The Final Words of Christ—lorn lamentation.
He played with whales and angels in *Creation*.

54. Mozart. Three of my violin teachers—Gerald Doty (of the Indiana University School of Music and University High School), Ede Zathureczky (see **29 Dohnányi**), and Daniel Guilet (of the Beaux Arts Trio)—assigned me three different violin concertos by W. A. Mozart. I'm predisposed to love him—always!

When Mozart awoke he'd be grabbing some paper

When Mozart awoke he'd be grabbing some paper—
Prepared for melodious morningtide caper:
    How *"zart"*—meaning "tender"— the way they'd
        approach!—
    The angels who came, when they Mozart would coach.

I know how he felt! We are taking dictation
Who, having attained an ascensional station
    In heaven-advance, leaving trouble behind,
    Are ready for travel in body and mind.

Dear Mozart, you played some duets with your sister:
I viewed how—exuberant, truly—you kissed her,
    O'erbrimmed with a bliss that you couldn't contain
    Received from the angel: writ down, 'twouldn't wane.

I need all the world to come dance with me! Hearing
In heart that the angels, unshaking, are speare-ing,
    Let's write and in canorous anthem rejoice,
    New hymn to put forth, in our angel-heard voice!

Happy Mozart's Birthday
for Zoja Pavlovskis
(1/27/13)

In Maynard Solomon's biography I've read
That many members of the family, instead
Of "Mozart," wrote it "Motzert." Let us grateful be
That fate the favored one more luckily had led!

It ought to be apparent—so it seems to me—
We need the "zart." Who ever wrote more "tenderly"?
Today abrasion rules in rude musician-heart:
The genial lyre prophetic—mute 'mid fiendish glee.

A holy, fine ideal is found, profound, in "zart"—
And, what is better yet, redeeming depth of "art"
We find contained therein, and in my name as well
(As you have shown me, lending thought a heady start).

Three teachers led me to that sweet melodic spell:
The G, D, A concerti heaven-tale would tell
That Mozart-loving men conveyed: what gift to me!
I'd join the group—a fourth—whom joy would swift impel.

And here's another Mozart lover—Albert Einstein!

Nonconformity—that's the key to living
reading Walter Isaacson, Einstein
(3/1/19)

Nonconformity—that's the key to living.
Albert, puzzled with something that resisted
Long, determined attempts at intellection,
      Played on the fiddle.

All at once, 'mid a lyric Mozart movement,
He'd exclaim, in a brash inventor-frenzy,
Caring not for the family or neighbors,
      "Yes!!" or "I've got it!!"

Maja entered the world—and baffled Albert.
Overcome by the toy-like apparition—
Keen observer, he looked at her, inquiring—
      "Where are the wheels, then?"

Bored with writing an eveningful of endnotes,
Gift I'm granted to jolt me from my stupor:
Albert, Isaacson, let me gladsome offer
      Thanks in profusion.

306 ♩ *Martin Bidney*

Do I get any smart-points for my spirit-kinship with Albert?
Here's additional praise for Mozart, the ever-young mentor of
speedy, spontaneous invention:

With the poems arriving beyond my control
(7/28/18)

With the poems arriving beyond my control
'Twere unwise to demur: I'd prefer to enroll
Every one in the site where memorial sprite
May abide, then arise, to my scions' delight.

I'm reminded, of course, of the soldiers of clay
That in China the folk who were digging one day
Had discovered, then gladly begun to unearth
Statues massively grand, of great sculptural worth.

That's a metaphor pleasant and fun to try out,
But it doesn't quite touch what my life is about:
Far too weighty and heavy, preparing for war,
These could never conceive what my writing is for.

I in spirit far more am to Mozart akin,
Who took orders each morn from the spirit within:
"Want to come on a walk? We'll just mosey along..."
"Maybe later—I'm sorry, I'm writing a song."

And here, interestingly, is a more extended interpretive
treatment of the B Minor Adagio considered briefly at the end
of **54 Mozart:**

The Adagio, B Minor, of Mozart in two
(9/1/18)

The Adagio, B Minor, of Mozart— in two
Parts divided—is measured, but—strange—breaking
   through

Contemplation of need for a stilling repose,
Fate required that emotion would conflict disclose.

The motifs he'll repeat as we heard them before,
But while grief's taking over, the freedom grows more
Uncontrolled, and the discipline needs to include
More of improvisation—new rhythms intrude.

Each idea's affirmed in a statement of thought
That, made sadder, great scope for a drama has wrought—
Yet, as if in a prayer, will balance be kept
For the feelings that altered when long they had slept.

For a few final measures a curtain drawn back
Turns the mood into major. Accustomed to lack
What of youth-time renewed would give tone to the rays
Of the light too long hidden, we're startled—and praise!

For me, the name "Mozart" sums up the joy of the "art" it
contains:

Spent years of my youth reading Pushkin and Goethe
(10/3/17)

Spent years of my youth reading Pushkin and Goethe,
Attention to melody ever alert, a
    Fine passion to catch when the рифмы текут
    Delighting the hearer, for счастие тут.

Entrancing the times when with ardor made fervent
I heard *glänzt die Sonne,* heart newly observant
    Cried out, in a frenzy enrapt, *lacht die Flur!*
    'Twas rhythm and rhyme made the pleasure so pure.

It seemed that in Eden, a deity speaking
Had found what he wanted, no need to go seeking:

You're pained when by dart of the Cupid-boy smit?
Sweet tunes will make Mozart-enjoyment of it.

I couldn't foresee that the day would befall me
When sky-dwelling angel by God-name would call me:
    Awake, yours the Poet-art: profit by this!
    Once tearful, pure sower-art reap, finding bliss.

In the following lyric, Mozart (with Bach) stimulates a combination of rhapsody, homily, and blessing:

Hearing Mozart, Quartet the Nineteenth, Part the Last
(9/6/18)

Hearing Mozart, Quartet the Nineteenth, Part the Last,
Then Third Keyboard Concerto, Bach's opener (fast
Were the both of them played—in each meaning of "light,"
Swift in spirit, and childlike as mind-smiling, bright)

I reverted to childhood, the time when to me
Were a sign and a wonder revealed—meaning He
(Not an angel, or seraph, or envoy) awoke
A procession that ended the mindset of yoke.

Oh, stay true to your soul, and explore what it tells:
From the rock in the desert where water upwells,
From the manna that falls like a merciful dew,
The Above, the Below will be nourishing you.

May the favor descend and the fountain arise,
Let the joy of the moistening shine in your eyes,
Be your hearing attuned to the fugue of our days
And the banner of lyric in thank-sign upraise.

    Here is an ecstatic moment when Mozart awakes the love of the soul (Solomon) for the Shekhinah or Indwelling Presence that in mystical Kabbalism is the Wisdom or Sophia Who, as Feminine Animating Principle, vitalizes the earth:

Mozart Music for a Solomonic Lover
sung in Binghamton University-Community Chorus,
Bruce Borton, Conductor
(2/7/12)

In *Vesperae solemnes de confessore* we hear
Laudate, pueri—Rejoice, you boys—a lesson dear
To him whose fate we jubilate, and likewise fine for Her
That as the theme of sweet rejoicing will the boy prefer.

Quis sicut Deus noster qui in altis habitat?
Shekhinah, and how queenly she! the heaven-sent *Shabbat.*
Humilia respicit—love's humility will bide
With him, her servitor, new-coronated by her side.

Et pauperum de stercore erigens: see the poor
From dunghill raised to glory with a love supreme and
     pure?
Forever let the lowly, O beloved, be redeemed,
Ascending thought begotten as creator-bliss beseemed!

O gentes omnes, populi, laudate Dominum!
Let more the heaven-lore extend, more angels, and more
     room.
The Wisdom where embodied all your blessing I may find
Let testify that Eden never died, Creator kind.

Of course, we needn't forget the comic, prankish aspect
of Mozart's fun-loving personality:

The Lighter Mozart
(8/21/16)

Two hundred thirty-one and -three
In Köchel-numbered canons bright
Bring *Proktophantasmist* to light—
But then he sings *Belle vierge Marie.*

In "Kyrie" a pious might
As in "Confiteor" I see.
Yet *Essen, Trinken* still must be
Twin themes that make him like to write.

"Du eselhafter Martin"? We
Decline to find here any slight...
In "Heil dem Tag" decisively

I want to prize the *Heiterkeit.*
Dear "Horch, ihr süßes Lied" is—whee!—
Like "Lebet wohl." And so, good night.

Mozart has a way of entering any of my memoir poems—at any time:

Lack of a topic? But how is that possible?
Massive the archive
(12/9/18)

Lack of a topic? But how is that possible? Massive the
　　archive
　　　　Waiting for one who would dare sample the treasury
　　　　trove!
Threescore fifteen were the years that encouraged the vast
　　compilation—
　　　　We'll of the visitor say, "Driven, determined, he dove!"

Pick a sensation at random. Your room? I am maybe
　　eleven...
　　　　Heading toward purple, the red—dreamer's linoleum
　　　　hue.
Look at the spider-web patterns of white—on the floor, I am
　　cutting
　　　　Essays with pictures from *Life*—art I will want to re-
　　　　view.

Turn to the bulky-big dresser, three drawers—how solid,
    enduring:
What is on top is the most crucial—my prized violin.
There it will rest—like an emblem of all that is best—on the
    altar.
    Mozart—*Concerto in G*—that's on the stand. Let's
    begin!

Colorful prints by Picasso, quite large, on the walls. *Three
    Musicians—*
That was the first of my loves. Then, *Casserole émaillée.*
Lastly, still life with the oranges, lemons and curious
    pitcher—
    Oh, and the *David* (Chagall), crowned, with his lyre set
    to play...

Old-fashioned timekeeper, pendulum steadily rightward
    and leftward—
    "Maelzel" had made it. I've since (many years afterward)
    learned
That was the name of the metronome company run by the
    man who
    Made one that Beethoven bought (happy distinction he
    earned!).

Sand-grain and wild-flower—Blake had proposed them for
    long contemplation.
    I the linoleum hue chose of the purple-red floor.
Wait—I had almost forgotten the map with the adage in
    Latin:
    "Borders that mortals have made—laughable—soon are
    no more."

Let's conclude with paired tributes to a Mozart composition
with solo violin, the D major "Trumpet concerto," which got
its name from the triumphant opening theme that, suddenly

and without notice, vanishes and never reappears! This is my favorite Mozart concerto, both for playing and for listening, and that's why I paid homage to it twice. First, an early sketch:

Wolfgang Amadeus Mozart
on a charcoal sketch of him by Aubrey Schwartz
(3/4/06)

The hinted clever humor of a boy—
A playfulness that meant he could forget
A clarion motif that had been set
To open a concerto. Like a toy

He dropped it, once the violin and strings
Had uttered—swift!—their "trumpet" melody—
His head was filled with other pageantry.
He lent his mind at once to genial things:

The glass harmonica Ben Franklin made;
A *Vogelfänger,* a Masonic rite;
To fugues by Bach new preludes; the delight
The Night Queen's pyrotechnic fire displayed.

And yet a keyboard slow-embroidered theme
Drew forth a happy-sad hypnotic dream.

And, next, a more developed presentation:

The "trumpet" concerto, the one in D major
(5/10/18)

The "trumpet" concerto, the one in D major,
Is deeply appealing to me, "golden ager,"
  Who, young, learned to play it on bold violin.
  With summons heraldic will Mozart begin!

Arpeggio triad—exhorting and forceful—
Yet such the supply the composer, resourceful,
    Can muster that after the call has been made,
    He other loved treasures will haste to unlade.

The call of the trump will Awakening blazon,
Yet after the dithyramb, brave diapason,
    'Tis wholly forgot and will never come back.
    Not oddly, we yet cannot notice the lack...

There's more—cornucopial store—than a hoarder
Could ever sort through in legitimate order
    With rule of the tools in the school to accord.
    Hear weltering welling, storms heavenly poured!

The horses of night, roaring forth in a thunder,
Will blinding arrive in their riving, a wonder:
    The wind that we breathe as we ride in our might
    Must from the Unmanifest come to the light.

55. Turkish Folk Music. Here's a reverie brought on by the experience of hearing a comparable folk performance:

Turco-Hebraic Dreaming
for Peter-Anton von Arnim
(7/5/07)

Ottoman-era sweet Ladino melodies—
I hear them on a perfect, warmly-sung CD
Brought, newly bought, from Turkey. Now it's bringing *me*
Back to the land of "might-have-been" hypotheses.

Strong urban singers with their vibrant ballads full
Of winding lines alive with trembling ornament—
A mere historic whim stopped *me* from being sent
By Isabel and Ferdinand to Istanbul.

We couldn't stay in Spain. So where, then, would we go?
Well, everywhere! We left! If chance had willed it so,
I'd now be singing languid chants in Turco-Spanish

With bits of Hebrew, Arabic, and even Greek.
It is another me I'd never meant to seek
But found, and that I now won't readily let vanish.

56. Ockeghem. I loved trying to imagine how the people felt who sang this Franco-Flemish music in the fifteenth century. I get a profound satisfaction from devotional states of mind. At the same time I had another thought which didn't quite get into the poem. Though the music was penned before Columbus ever set sail, in the year 2019 it taxes my thinking capacity to the limit, and I can't quite follow the counterpoint. Shouldn't my education have prepared me to understand this pre-modern piece?

57. British Folk Music. The group Nowell Sing We Clear performed annually during the Christmas season in upstate NY at Binghamton's Cranberry Coffeehouse. My poem employs the unusual wordsong form of the first folk number on their CD, with entirely new words.

58. Beethoven. The finest poem I ever read about this melody-titan is by poet Nikolai Zabolotsky (1903-1958). I derived the text from a public domain site and have translated it, in form-true mode, for you. (That means, among other things, that the sudden hexameters in lines 3 and 4 are the poet's own.)

Nikolai Zabolotsky, "Beethoven" tr. MB
Бетховен (1946)

The very day your concords overcame
A world where efforts generated are,
Light overpowered light, passed cloud through cloudy frame,
Thunder advanced on thunder, star moved into star.

An inspiration wild your mind would seize:
In orchestras of thunder-trembling storm
You, rising by nephelial degrees,
Touched music of the worlds with gesture warm.

By trumpet groves, lakes melody-enspelled,
Unwieldy shapeless hurricanes you'd tame.
Into the face of Nature's self you yelled:
Through organ tones your lion visage came.

Before the face of all the world expanse
You so much thought in that vast cry could place
That word surged through the world it would enhance
And turned to music, wreathed the lion face.

Again the bull-horned lyre will loud resound,
A shepherd flute be formed of eagle bone:
You understood the life-charmed world around
And good walled off from evil, using tone.

And through the calm of world-extending space
Up to the very stars—the ninth great wave!—
Be opened, Thought! From Music, word, gain grace!
Pound, livened heart! And peace in triumph save!

Here is my own attempt at a comparable tribute:

Beethoven and Goethe's *Faust*
(4/21/12)

*to Katharina Mommsen with deepest gratitude
for her gift of Beethoven's* opera omnia *on CDs*

Boïto couldn't do it, nor could bland Gounod.
There's only one who might the epic set in tone
That Goethe by his life had equaled. He alone
Possessed the range and scope with spirit wing to go

Where Ganymede-Prometheus-Muhammad went:
Beethoven—stormy Faustian sforzando-burst!
Decision burdensomely made—yet he's the first
That to Romantic passion classic shape had lent.

Homuncular, a receptivity would grace
The country symphony, the violin *Romance*
In F that would my teenage happiness enhance.
Two themes, he claimed, "religion, and the thoroughbass,"

He'd never speak about: Mephistophelian scorn
Arose in him when pompous dogmas offered were.
And yet—Eternal Female—he resembled Her
In empathetic *Ode to Joy*, from heaven borne.

    To another friend, I addressed other lyrical thoughts on
the topic:

Goethe and Beethoven: A Sonnet
for Charlene Thomson
(10/28/07)

The souls that form a standard for the judgment of
The work of later age's creativity
Need patience. Had he waited for a century
Goethe would find that East-West testament of love

He'd published not sold out! The riddle rose above
Customers' comprehension. Undespairingly
He labored, though. A Noah, from a darkened sea
He'd send a helpful essay out, a hopeful dove.

Beethoven's *Grosse Fugë* was rejected. He
Who'd conquered chaos might have beckoned equably
To future angels of a more evolved assent.

Guarneri players, mainly in their seventies,
Have with a vintaged wisdom stranger empathies
Than we can guess. For them the message had been meant.

And—of course—here are a couple of poems on Beethoven's
Ninth. First comes the experience I had as tenor participant
in performing Beethoven's triumphal Ninth in Binghamton
University-Community Choir under the direction of Bruce
Borton. The choir stood right behind the orchestra, and I liked
watching the instrumentalists warm up:

Dress Rehearsal, Beethoven's Ninth
(11/14/09)

Deine Zauber binden wieder
Was die Mode streng geteilt...

A trumpet, or a horn, may silver be, or gold.
Bassoons are leaning leftward; of the double bass
Three players like the German way to hold the bow,
The fourth prefers the French. I'm watching all the hands

Adapt themselves. Rodin would help you to behold
Uncommon curves with new awareness of their grace;
The melodies recall the roads where they would go
In former time. The trio-pastoral commands

A glance before the scherzo-ending. To unfold
The pre-ode travel map, three backward looks take place
Within the Bachian recitative, whose flow
Leads deeplier to hymning joy. One understands

The startling Turkish march, impulsive rhythm shifts,
Joining what custom sundered, healing spirit-rifts.

Next, a re-write of the "Ode to Joy." In fact, with slight
adaptations, my version can be sung to the Beethoven melody:

Beethoven's Ninth
(2/20/08)

Music is an optimism.
That's why hymning "An die Freude"
Helps the rhapsode to avoid a
Bleakness of the blank abysm.

Cosmic optimysticism
Waving in the rainbow prism,
God-in-us en-thu-siasm
Gladly clambers up the chasm.

Falling at the thyrsal altar
Thirsting for the Bacchus fountain,
Climb the Dionysus mountain.
Fire-drunk, never let us falter.

Frenzied, fear no paroxysm,
Ardor-harm, or fever-spasm:
By the ocean-protoplasm
Be with music fused in chrism.

Here's another of my love-struck tributes to the "Ode to Joy":

We by flame inebriated to your sanctuary come
on a line from "An die Freude" by Friedrich Schiller:
"Wir betreten, feuertrunken, Himmlische, dein Heiligtum"
(12/14/17)

"We by flame inebriated to your sanctuary come":
Here a scene is replicated to a Dionysian drum.
God the Father, great, exalted, Whom we laud to full extent,
Dwells above the spacious, vaulted, ever-during starry tent.

Blessed Joy, who come to us in likeness of a freedom-light,
Freude-Freiheit, you of custom-limits make the spirit bright.
Siblings we of one another chant Your praise the world
    around:
Where your vasty pinions hover Joy and Life alike are
    found.

"We to you our heart surrender, offering your glory praise":
That's how Tyutchev's rendering in Russian would the
    thought rephrase,
Taking out the drunken triumph, humbler making what we
    do:
He no longer as "Elysium's daughter" would envision you.

You of God, "great Father," are the daughter in the altered
    chant,
And with hints of Church Slavonic for a priestly hierophant,
You in form a little changing, as may suit the Russian ear,
Nonetheless through nations ranging ever more our souls
    endear.

Joy, I'm grateful daily, for my heart most loves in hymn and
    psalm
High and deep to hail ye whether felt in chaos or in calm:
Every organ I possess and every thought that comes to
    mind
Join the skiey choir to bless what you have wrought and
    soul divined.

A Goethe poem set by Beethoven, which we sang in
University-Community Chorus conducted by Bruce Borton,
appealed to me so much I translated it to bring across the
uniquely metered, sweetly rhymed music that stirred the
composer:

For Beethoven's Meeresstille und glückliche Fahrt, Op. 112
Calm Sea and Prosperous Voyage
translated from Goethe's German by MB

Water ruled by deepest quiet,
Mute becalmed unmoving sea—
Boatsman vainly busied by it,
Surface will but smoother be.
Not a breeze from any quarter,
Ocean deadly silent lies!
Monsterlike the widened water,
Never will a wave arise.

    The cloudlets are riven,
    The heaven is bright—
    By Aeolus driven,
    All fear taking fright.
    The wind is upsurging,
    The boatsman well-guided,
    Fast, faster! the urging—
    The waves are divided.
    A gift is emerging—
    The land is in sight!

On a light note, the following poem makes a little joke about the question and answer—"Must it be?" "It must be"—written by Beethoven in the MS. margins of his quartet No. 16 in F Major, Op. 135, which I've played with friends:

Beethoven Quartet
(8/7/16)

The cat of black and white that lies
In fiddle case—O nap divine!—

Were I to ask it, "Muß es sein?"
Might answer me with tranquil eyes

In quiet tone, "Es muß!" The wise
Reply made clear to ears like mine
Mere "Mew!" might seem, with tone condign,
To those who cat-speech can't apprise.

Late Ludwig brewed a vintage fine:
Our feline friend can realize,
If dimly, what a dervish wine

Can mean to one who skyward sighs:
'Twill mew to music and recline
And freedom feel in mind arise.

59. Liszt. Though the composer sub-headed the masterly work "After a reading of Dante," the annotations have helpfully made it clear that what he had focused on in that reading was the story of Paolo and Francesca, lured into illicit romance when reading together a pander-book about Launcelot and now forever whirled together in a hellish tempest, a perfect dream-emblem combination-compromise of love and punishment, desire and fear.

60. Brahms. This tonal visionary resembles Handel in linking joy to nobility:

Thy Glory, Titan
(5/29/06)

It's happened now for years, repeatedly,
But now, in Brahms' new opus thirty-four—
Familiar in quintet arrangement, more
Percussive here—two keyboard players—free

To pound, relentless, flying fingers down
To strike upon the glory-chords—the cry
That crowns the shout of laughter, rising high
And irrepressible! A concert-clown

I might be called, for at a climax I
Desire to laugh, and when it's done, I do.
I couldn't wait the whole conclusion through
In this, the Brahms, but laughed into the sky.

Great music makes me laugh, it looses me.
I'm glad to be alive—I'm glad *to be*.

Here is a quiet piece:

Intermezzi
(8/21/16)

Brahms' opus hundred seventeen
He wrote as woe-born lullabies:
Each tune when gentle baby cries
Will shape a childhood dream serene.

"I'm grieved to see your weeping eyes:
Dream softly, sweetly"—hymn he'd seen,
A "Song of Scotland," pure, pristine.
In perfect Herder book it lies:

World Folksong Voices. Wave marine:
I violinned the windy sighs.
The flowing, rolling waters keen

As any mother might surmise
Who'd want a starry ocean queen
To join the keening, holy, wise.

And here is a companion piece for it:

Johannes Brahms
on a charcoal drawing of him by Aubrey Schwartz
(3/2/06)

There is an openness about the man,
Arising when the joys of intellection
Join with an asking look of introspection—
The large dark pupils noting both—and can

We doubt that he is waiting, wondering
Whether the phrase now forming in his head
(One eyebrow quizzically raised) had led
To something unexpected? Will he sing

The melody that might be coming soon?
The mouth is rounded, and the lips are pursed,
Prepared to sound a note. The hearer versed
In Brahmsian transitions where the tune

Is major-minor, uncommitted, strange,
Will find that roving mind, that open range.

And here, in a letter to a friend, I transcribe one of my
most impassioned experiences of rehearsing Brahms in choir.

On the Prospect of Receiving a Novella
for Philipp Restetzki
(10/26/10)

I'd like to get a story based on Brahms!
Tonight, in choir, we sang his *Schaffe mir.*
Techniques of Palestrina will appear
In this motet that anguishes, then calms.

Ein reines Herz und einen neuen Geist!
Verwirf mich nicht—we hear the spirit-qualm,

Then *Tröste mich mit deiner Hülfe*—balm
And balsam, with a heav'n aroma spiced.

Der freud'ge Geist erhalte mich—enticed
By hope from Luther's well-beloved psalm
That to the careworn came, assuaging fear,

He'd win, at length, tranquillity of AUM
And, rapidly advanced to higher sphere,
Would find himself, at last, emparadised.

(Note: Philipp did send the Brahms-related narrative he
wrote, and I thoroughly relished it!) It is good to have friends
with whom one may, in letters, treat such topics: indeed,
Philipp and I are co-authors of a bilingual book dedicated to
friendship itself! The title is *Ein nie geahntes Vergnügen / A
Treat Not Known Before.*

For an all-Brahms evening, our Binghamton Downtown
Singers, conducted by Kristi Ruffo, offered a threefold
presentation:

Liebeslieder Walzer, Gesang der Parzen, Triumphlied
(4/30/18)

So long had I taught—yet the glow becomes duple,
For now I'm remorphed as a quick-learning pupil
    More eager than ever the teacher to please
    And letting the wind-sprite enliven the breeze.

Each love song a waltz, all eighteen of them charming—
We learn them in German. The fate-ode's alarming
    Where Goethe the Underworld shows in a dirge
    When titans from punishment mighty emerge.

Big hymn—double chorus with baritone solo—
The *"Triumphlied"*—splendid! *Placēre nunc volo*—

The better we sing, more the Master we laud.
(So children are thrilled when their parents applaud.)

With stouthearted power then let's be attuning
(Atoning, at-one-ing) our tone, by repugning
    All flaws while refining our triumph in June,
    An homage to Brahms for the musical boon.

I even quote Kristi Ruffo in the poem that follows—a tribute to the faith and confidence of a superbly competent and heartening conductor. The harmonies in Brahms' *Love Song Waltzes* are so ingenious, and so unfamiliar, that we at times appeared to need the encouragement she so memorably offered. And think about it: how can 18 waltzes in a row avoid a feeling of monotony? Only the gods know the answer, and they imparted it to Brahms. She was resoundingly right: the songs are all gorgeous—and each in a different way.

The happy custom I've achoired
(2/19/18)

The happy custom I've achoired
Of weekly song with others, wired
To get the most from Brahms, who brings
Repeated treats. I may be tired,

It may be late—and yet there springs
A blithe desire to tell some things
That happen every time I go
To practice. What a spirit wings

Around the room! The music-flow
As on a stream with sparkle-show
I view—the bright, ignited gaze
Of choristers and leader. Slow

Or fast the tempo, each will raise
A deep-felt need to speak the praise
Of one who swayed by waltzing wrote
What eighteen times true love portrays.

The wand'ring harmonies, I note,
Might startle, as a wave the boat
May at an angle strike, and stir
Some bafflement—and yet we float

Ahead: whatever may occur,
We'll keep in mind the words of her
Who said, "Fear not, I guarantee
'Twill all be beautiful!"—a spur

To further noble effort! We
Doubt not the truth of that. Agree?
No dances have I more admired
Than these I sing and hearing see.

To conclude, I interpret one of the noblest and most invigorating works of my beloved Brahms:

Brahms' *Variations on a Theme "of Haydn"*
(5/25/06)

(1)

It is the life-hymn of a happy man:
Theme rich in grace, the brave *St. Anthony
Chorale* played lieder-like and tenderly.
Sweet pauses, gentle hesitancy can

Prepare us for initial venturing
Where soft three-quarter calm, a cradle-motion,
Is punctuated, far above the ocean-
Wave-interweaving, by the bell-bright ring

Of a repeated high note, with a phrase
Made from the hymn, as if an infant tried
To imitate it, promptly gratified
By the reply approving of his ways.

Livelier dotted rhythms introduce
Outburst, assertion, mooring coming loose.

(2)

After that variant, the mood calms down:
Walk on an autumn day, *andante*-pace.
Two notes arising, two descending, place
The mind in balance. But a louring frown

Brought on a brief depression, wonderment,
Weariness, all uncomprehended. Then,
Directionless, wild energy of men
Dancing—a tarantella?—may be meant

To show a quick recuperative force;
For hunter, drum and trumpet, steady beat
Ensue, a measured racing, little heat:
We're riding on a fine, triumphant horse!

Now ends an epoch. Love awakening,
A light-filled riddle will begin to sing.

(3)

Yet cloud and wind-lash overspread the face
Of dim, brow-troubled moon in minor key
Followed by two-three mixture-meter. We
Hear a decision forming, making place

For unawaited feeling that will be
Part of a grand expanding. Now: a dance,

Relaxing breather from hard circumstance—
Mustering wayward thought, determinedly.

All dared, all done! The final figuration,
Ascending scale, affirming rapid rise,
Mounting, repeats. We, grateful, raise our eyes—
The loved chorale's come back—with jubilation—

The emblematic energy of Brahms
Heightened, exciting even while it calms.

61. Barber. "Adagio for Strings," which I had the chance
to play in the original string quartet version—in five flats—is
so eternally-perfect that it really shocked me, one day, to think
that my parents grew up never having heard it:

Samuel Barber
(9/19/08)

A shock the sudden thought: my parents, till their late
Twenties could never hear "Adagio for Strings"!
It was a work of nineteen thirty-six—to be
Surprised at anything so plain should make me smile.

And yet it felt uncanny! Automatic: while
You feel or hear a work of beauty ever great,
Imagination puts it in eternity;
Perfection dwells among imperishable things.

Value immaculate, that wholly fills our mental space,
Grandly expands into the total time of soul.
And quite the same with what we loathingly bewail:
Our sorrow is the world; how can it then pass by?

And people kill themselves who can't abide the place
Called Pain, the time called Woe—combined, unending
   whole.

Or they'll design a heaven blest, unending sky,
Where love alone abides and ever will avail...

My second poem on this will I hope clarify the way Barber's contemplative, transporting work became one of the central meaning-giving powers in my life:

I want to write what never wasn't there
(4/3/19)

I want to write what never wasn't there.
Before the world was made we saw it fair.
"Adagio for Strings" when Barber penned,
The heart was widened, holy might to bear.

That only I'd inscribe which will remain.
I crave in simple word a sacred strain.
We need no more beginning, nor an end.
For all is with us, and our aim is plain.

I need to sing what couldn't not exist.
The tearless eyes that smile by sky are kissed.
Beyondness, kind imponderable friend,
Our view has with a mercy dew emblissed.

To chant I pray as when the heaven wooed
That psalmer with a longing sigh endued
Which through entire creation would extend
And blessed the best beloved it pursued.

Barber, for me, is a psalmer. The slow movement played is the sigh of a longing lover. It wanders the universe to bless and laud the best belov'd of all of us: the Omnifingent Who, in Sufi thought, brought our worlds into being through the single breath of a solitary, yearning sigh, in order that the beloveds created in this manner could return the love bestowed.

62. Stravinsky. I hoped to intimate the extreme originality
of the man in this poem:

Third Symphony
(5/25/17)

Third Symphony: if no one had told of war,
Nor uttered thought of tyrant or liberties,
      We wouldn't be requiring guidance
    Through the Stravinskyan thinking pattern.

Unprecedented, maybe, the rhythm strength,
Whose main appeal is balance of planned with strange—
      Insistent, yet accommodating,
    Every assertion with person-power.

Yet added to simplicity of motif
Are timbres rich as any an empire graced:
      Had Rimsky-Korsakov not written,
    Half of the color I feel were absent.

The sudden introduction of novel hues
In wand'rings of complexity never dreamed
      With distant relatives acquaint us,
    Quickly arrived and as soon departed.

And in the following tribute I give voice to the feeling he lends
me of supreme playfulness, a comic bravura as of Picasso:

In the colorful *Agon* Stravinsky has writ

In the colorful *Agon* Stravinsky has writ
    Where's the "struggle" depicted? 'Tis fit
That we answer by listening. That is the place
    Where a conflict Olympic we face.

In the mini-length parts, the announcer averred,
    Might a host of composers be heard
From baroque and the classic Mozartean age
    Until Schoenberg, Boulez take the stage.

One astonishing thing from the start is made clear:
    Ovewhelming's the unity here.
Though admittedly bombs at tradition he lobs,
    Each attack, as in *Calvin and Hobbes,*

Is a playful aggression, a six-year-old's claim
    For the polymorph id to find aim.
Though Olympian track-meets with fury were fierce
    Yet did poets compete. They'd transpierce,

Each with hymn to the lyre, every vaunted desire
    That a rival might stir to aspire:
In competitive rivalry, height is the prize
    To be sought by the strong and the wise.

Thus in *Agon* the tone-colors, altering, rouse
    With a startle most artful. And how's
The engagement of hearers in changeful events
    To be kept both attentive and tense?

Well, the tender and soft to the strident in pride
    Are adjoined and in form are allied:
With a witty-quick balance of conflict and play
    Comic mindset is making its way.

Because the mindset of Stravinsky is so overpoweringly life-asserting, as I feel it, the varied rationales for *Rite of Spring* that feature a predominance of alleged desire to die seem to me incompatible with what really goes on. Indeed, not death and dissolution but life and triumph are also the legacy of shaman performances, which continue to be practiced worldwide:

Rite of Spring?—I have learned that
the girl hadn't died
hearing the Stravinsky work performed on two pianos
(10/20/18)

Rite of Spring?—I have learned that the girl hadn't died.
She had whirled as a dervish and firmly relied
On the god of the morning who, vernal, returned
And, outpouring rewarding, had spermed her unspurned.

In their sorcery centuries earlier, too,
Had the maidens that fainted in mercy come through
Guaranteed that their blood would by none be required
When to flood their new being with Sun they desired.

When the priest had with osculant zeal given earth
His profession of faith in a forthcoming birth,
Katabasis would high anastasis imply:
He with blessing had promised the girl wouldn't die.

Little death? To be blest. Greater death? To be shunned.
On our flame-stream the highest of light-rays have sunned.
With particulate energy all of us whirl—
I'm a dervish no less than the light-favored girl.

63. Lully. We owe a great deal to this lucky, inventive, and powerful man for having encouraged lively syntheses of opera, comedy, and dance at the Court of Louis XIV in Versailles.

64. Weinberger. My grade-school music teacher was more widely educated than I had ever guessed; Weinberger became a highlight experience of my younger years, yet few people that I know have ever heard of him.

65. Boyce. I celebrated him thirteen years ago:

The Growing Violinist
(1/2/06)

For teenage-time baroque is ever best.
Enjoy the boyishness of William Boyce
(The well-named), and the energetic voice
And driving urgings from Vivaldi. (Test

The playful sweep of Haydn, Mozart, next:
Amid the humor, pathos.) Handel and
Corelli, Telemann, with open, grand,
So-lung-expanding breathing, to a text

Of scripture finely suited, give the player
Acquaintance with a rooted harmony,
Firm, solid, large as ample cedar tree,
Of upright age the sign, in David's prayer.

But Bach! Behold the man. A greater one
Was never known below the waking sun.

66. Bruch. Learning to play his invigorating concerto for violin was one of my major formative experiences, even though the double-stopped ascending tenths in the third movement convinced me irrefutably that I could not become a concert violinist. Bruch is such a gifted melodist that I once heard his freely creative arrangement of "Kol Nidrei" played at a Reform Jewish Day of Atonement service not along with, but *instead of,* a recitation of the prayer.

67. Burns. I have written the quoted refrain from Burns' poem as it is sung on the record; thus instead of "gardener" I write "gärdner." A "paidle" is a hoe or spade, according to *The Canongate Burns: The Complete Poems and Songs of Robert Burns,* ed. Andrew Noble and Patrick Scott Hogg (Edinburgh, UK: 2001) 326.

It may be stretching things a bit to call Burns a composer

since generally he set his lyrics to folk tunes, but the superb poetry he wrote for the music has helped lend world popularity to the Scottish songs. One of my own singing favorites for years has been "Ye Banks and Braes of Bonnie Doon"; I've performed it often while accompanying myself on violin. As Martin Luther famously adopted popular tunes when setting the hymns he composed, so in Britain Charles Wesley, brother of John the founder of the Methodist Church, set to the tune of "Ye Banks" a hymn of his own composition, "Come, O Thou Traveler Unknown," #387 in *The United Methodist Hymnal* (Nashville TN: United Methodist Publishing House, third printing 1989). It has 14 stanzas. I think I will perform it (or at least half of it) soon, for, as John Wesley averred, "Dr. [Isaac] Watts did not scruple to say that 'that single poem, Wrestling Jacob, was worth all the verses he himself had written'" (note to #387).

Lovers of Scottish culture may enjoy the following joke:

Minstrelsy of the Scottish Border
for Charlene Thomson
(4/16/08)

Today, as I was doing, just for fun,
A short Lyceum course, with a musician
Who loved the Scottish musical tradition,
She told some jokes; and here, for you, is one.

When God created Scotland, he had done
A thing that, by the angels' own admission,
Expressed unprecedented ebullition,
Granting abundance of each benison.

The dewy, heather-covered, misty hills,
And sheep and goats, and mead where shepherd basked,
With banks and braes, pink thistle, frith, and rills,

Made God contented with his grateful labors.
"Haven't you been *too good* to Scotland?" asked
An angel. "No. You never met their neighbors."

And perhaps lovers of Celtic music, like my fellow folk
musicians Tim and Johanna, might be cheered by this light-
hearted item:

Sonnet for Johanna and Tim Masters
(4/8/08)

The Muse commands me, and I serve her daily
(I'd even write for Prairie Home Companion).
Blithe as a wilding Scottish capercaillie,
I'll spawn a sonnet, modest frolic fanion.
No need to go across a yawning canyon
(Although she'd likely aid me, gladly, gaily),
Nor braid my line as Adam's branching banyan,
But simply sing, as in a choiring ceilidh.
My lured computer now for minstrel spinning
Is turned into a harp with heartstring sighing;
I'm angeled by the shaking of the winning
Winds from the birded flinging time that's flying,
    With feather-ankled step, mad cap, and thyrse.
    Down from a cloud-bar, see!—click-sprinkled verse.

68. Scriabin. Here's a verse comment on the Russian
experimental seeker, occasioned when I played trio movements
with cellist Dietrich Brandt and pianist Marcos Kopf at a
birthday celebration for Katharina Mommsen in Weimar.
Marcos played splendid solos, which I commemorate and
praise:

To Marcos Kopf
(10/26/10)

It's nine-twelve Taylor Drive, in Vestal, in New York.
I'd love to get a picture, bringing back alive

A memory, as by the spirit-filling drive
Achieved that splendid lent a rolling whirlwind torque

Of motion over keys that flew too quick to see;
A Russian poet when he heard Scriabin claimed
The will he bodied forth could not be rightly named:
The elf had turned a giant, spraying waves in glee.

The force of nature that creates our classic art
Will hide that skill in semblance of a primal power
Which is indeed the Will evoked by Schopenhauer.

Recalling how you played will make the beating heart
Pound louder and the lungs breathe deeper and the tongue
And lips of poet stir till lauds in awe be sung.

The "Russian poet" mentioned was Konstantin Dmitrievich
Balmont (1867–1942), to whose laudation of Scriabin I allude
in the following two poems which I translate from Balmont's
Russian:

(1) **Great and Doomed** [Великий Обреченный]

He felt the world in form of symphonies
And into floating temple forth would pour
Touch, incense, tone, processionals galore
With dancing, finer emblem-congeries—

The shine of summer, bloom, solarities,
All lunar fortune-telling, starry lore,
A whisper and a thunder, less and more,
And odd, auroral-teasing melodies.

'Midst earthly dream, awaking into sky,
Bestrowing whirlwind-sparks that fog transpierce,
In gleam of sacrifice unfrightened, fierce—

And in the flaming maw enwound so high,
Awoken into death, a soul that glows...
Mad elf, inviting, urging, Scriabin rose.

(2) **Elf [Эльф]**

At first the fairies played in lunar light.
Male major, female minor—striving twain—
Portrayed, combined, the kiss and then the pain.
And, after little stirrings on the right,

At left erupted tones of wizard-might.
A Will sang out twin blended wills—their strain.
Bright Elf, the monarch of accordant gain,
Carved cameos, thin, delicate and slight—

Then countenances, whirled in current-sound,
Each glimmering in golden, steely gleam,
Replaced the joy with tristful woe extreme.

The crowds came on, with choral thunders 'round.
And God to Man the Doppelgänger seemed.
Scriabin at the grand piano dreamed.

69. Ravel. Here's a little sketch I penned (why did I use that poetic diction? It misleads: in real life I write wordsongs only on the computer) in response to a portrait I admired:

Maurice Ravel
on a charcoal portrait of him by Aubrey Schwartz
(5/9/06)

We hear a sea-borne breeze, a wind-borne wave,
The speaking leaves and sudden sunshine he
Portrays, with ease and unexpectedly,
When briskly guiding us to view the *Grave*

Of Couperin, recalling *Ocean Boat*.
And then, the *Minuet in Antique Style*
Another theme brings in, for all the while
The sweetly carven melodies he wrote

Appear in dream—the spell of *Mother Goose,*
Far more than childlike, blends all purities
Of woodwind timbres—with an Eden-ease
Bolero and *La Valse*—Help! Demons loose!

But when the tale is ancient, in *Pavane
For Dead Infanta*, perfect love is won.

70. de Falla. The extreme beauty of the sweet concord, made spicy with contrasting dissonance when fit, made me want to pay tribute in a meter tightly harmonized. So I selected an Omar-like strophe that I varied, changing aaxa bbxb (unrhymed third line in each quatrain) to aaba bbcb (third line as preview of the three more to come in the following stanza). Sudden little alterations in the rhythm, too, may, I hope, accord with the unexpected rhythmic elements in de Falla's exploration venture.

71. Fanny Mendelssohn. I'll offer a dialogic response to more of her songs:

Six *Lieder* by Fanny Mendelssohn
(9/19/09)

Hear not a mere accompanist at the piano
Fulgent in surging current-figuration, full
Of blended weather of the wind and sea, a pull
In wave and air and sun exerted: the soprano

A floating bird above the mirror-light that wells
Fulgurant while the eye-exciting blinding gleam
Has turned the cresting breakers hyaline, wild stream
Fervent in pre-creation chaos that foretells

The eye and mind that later will ascend to see:
Here's Eichendorff transformed. The winter Heine-tree
Sad hammer will endure of Thor until a dream

Reveal an eastern palm in deeper sleep—where teem
The stormy runes of ancient North—or are they bells
At midnight? Mystery of intermelded spells...

    72. Wolf and Mörike. Here is my own "Hugo Wolf moment":

Morning Thoughts on Hugo Wolf
reading Harold C. Schonberg, Lives of the Great Composers
(4/11/12)

Wild write-a-song career: confined to seven years!
I've been a poet, it appears, for nearly eight.
In me, the daimon drove the whirling soul elate,
With every day the first, for sky dawn-cloven clears

The prospect nightly reached when I, with waning sun—
By sounding silence bowed, like the Enshrouded One
Whom Allah respite gave, and heartened rest far more
Than day might gain—by Houri guided had begun,

In starlight that for me would then disclose a door,
To let the harp, the barbiton within outpour
What strengthened Hugo Wolf to do what he had done:
The dark, the lumen-liminal, the metaphor.

Incisive *write* relates to rip and rive and rend,
And *chant* is Greek *eikános*: here the rooster cries.
The Lord in shining sky will oracle the eyes:
We may go mad at last, yet view a lasting Friend.

    73. Borodin. Here are some thoughts on his surprising
Bachian cello-piano venture:

Borodin, Cello Sonata
(10/5/07)

Or should the title be "Sonata by
Bach for the Violin, with Fugue G Minor"?
You couldn't find a meditation finer
On that recurrent stirring theme that I

Had played with relish as an awestruck boy,
Although the notes were unaccompanied,
My youthful hands too small (they're so, indeed,
In age) for triple stopping. Slavic joy

Made all the lightsome, jolly cello and
Piano dialogue a fond exchange
Of married memories of narrow range

Repeated, altered. Final part—a waltz!
Accelerating motion only halts
To claim the theme, become both glad and grand.

74. Reger. Tribute to a brilliant music maker:

Max Reger—solo cello, a triple suite
(5/29/17)

Max Reger—solo cello, a triple suite,
A trinal opus: here we can watch him grow.
        But even at the start I see a
Youthful delight in the fugal writing.

We gladly pause to ponder the marvel-deed:
A polyphonic feast for the cello? Yes!
        The man I thank who dared to tackle
Challenge with valor—O sing the hero!

Praeludiums with pleasure the heart relax
Before the dances leap that abound in play
      And when Andante comes to wander
    All of the variants lead to wonder.

When Pater claimed that song is the aim of art
He prophesied what here I would fain attempt:
      Loved tones of English, mother-music,
    Wing me the speed of a cupid-arrow!

Reger has given me some of my happiest moments in chamber
music playing: the harmonies in the two largos that Frieda
and I loved are transcendent:

Max Reger
to the treasured memories of John and Frieda Flint
(12/19/05)

They say, reacting to a mean review,
He wrote a famous letter, saving face:
"I'm reading it in a secluded place;
It's right before me now, but in a few

Moments I'll put the thing behind me." Well,
Who had the final word? We rarely hear
The work of Reger now, but a severe
Critique is out of place. I cannot tell

You how transformative the largos are
That he included in sonatas for
Piano, violin—stalactites, or
Polypoid coral. Chord-hues glimmer far

Away from anything we'd ever known:
He'd ventured on strange feeling-seas, alone.

75. Moussorgsky. In an unusual procedure, I would like to pay tribute to a Russian poet whose lyrics inspired perfect songs by the composer. First I will translate a poem, then offer a dialogic verse "reply" offering the Moussorgskyan context.

In a Hut by Arseny Goleníshchev-Kutuzov (1848–1913)

Lonely, dark along my farther way.
Evening twilight deep, disheartening.
Just one single sadly wavering
Roadside glimmer-flame amid the gray.

Now I'll come in closer: covered in
Snow, a simple little hamlet stands.
At the border of the blackened lands,
In a squalid hut, that fire burns thin.

Who, then, in the ever darker night
Stays awake—and why?—to view the sight?
And—whose shadow in the window pane?

None can tell. The troika speeded past.
Empty, humanless, again—so fast!—
All is dark, disheartening—again!

Reply to Golenishchev-Kutuzov

Writing for Moussorgsky mordant songs—
Dances, too, of death—and then a set
Labeled plainly *Sunless* cannot let
Any *lieder* connoisseur who longs

For a change of aura chase it down
Readily in such a poet's lines.
Yet if you would favor subtle signs

Here you find them. His, the twilight crown

For a nocturne of a perfect make.
What will not— and can't—be said will take
More account of what, unspoken, we've

Come to know about the way a fire
Darkens all around until desire
Might resolve on something to believe.

76. Martinů. See **29 Dohnányi** for a mention of this composer.

77. Saint-Saëns. Here's a tribute to him:

Saint-Saëns
(4/19/12)

(1)

The radio announcer gave the players' name:
The Rembrandt Trio. The composer? No, too late...
My pleasant curiosity would not abate:
To Mendelssohn akin, and her of less acclaim,

Sky-favored sibling of that wonder-child, I felt
The one to be who sang in lilting lyric strain
With keyboard-play cascading: simple the refrain,
A five-note dotted-rhythm, elegant and svelte.

The ballad next: could it be Schumann? Could it be
His wife? Her compositions I have come to love.
The partly-pizzicato scherzo humor showed

That Schubert might have liked. Well-trodden scenic road
The fine melodic soul had traveled, mindful of
Romanticism active, and it puzzled me.

(2)

The Trio in F Major by Saint-Saëns! I learned
It had been written in his twenties' youthful mood.
I'd never thought he'd been so fruitfully endued
By trio-masters that his early homage earned.

I like him better, now I know his "family."
The work, as fresh as if it had been penned today,
Is, too, a new acquaintance who as friend will stay
A treasured being gladly met and blest, for me.

A gardener the winter snowdrop will applaud:
Announcer of the spring. And we who keep the field
Of Eden that is human feeling shaped in art

Are by the sprouting, sourcing, comparably awed
That heart and mind to the creator daily yield
In form aborning. Draw the *álif.* Make a start.

78. Messiaen. Stimulated by his *Catalogue of Birds* for piano, I compared Messiaen to other great visionaries:

Rouault, Redon, Messiaen
(9/8/13)

The gems that struggle through the dark,
Unwilled, impelled to gleam, will mark
Incursion of the otherwhere
That those enheartened rise who hark

To starting flood when jewel rare
Emerges from oneiric air—
As, too, Redon will, fevered, show
In boat-floor beams of carmine glare,

Or harsh unworldly turquoise glow.
Surprised are we, who likewise grow
By Messiaen astonished: he
In *Catalogue of Birds* made flow

Craved canticle—crazed melody—
In laud of birds by God set free.
O third of Sufis! whom Rouault
Called forth, adored in prophecy.

Another of my moments of Messiaenic transport:

I'm starting to grasp how friend Pushkin is feeling
(3/28/18)

I'm starting to grasp how friend Pushkin is feeling
Whenever his rhymes by the yard he's unreeling
    Or (changing the metaphor) praising the flow
    Of rhythms that swing—Hail-Farewell!—as they go.

He's coming to mind in the quiet ensuing
When still I am filled by the impulse accruing
    From gifts that I serially have received,
    For he who believes will be never bereaved.

I go to the door and, retrieving the paper,
Hear tunes—four, six, eight—every present a shaper
    Of multiple meters that blend in the brain:
    They merge Messiaenic, each fervent refrain!

Refreshing as well is the dew while I'm striding
On green, soft and moist, where the paper's abiding:
    No longer delivered, it merely is thrown—
    Yet greetings are many, you're never alone.

The French composer comes to mind often! Birds are major
in my life, and Messiaen is my guide to their polyrhythms
and multi-tonalities:

Observing beauty in unlikely spots
(3/21/18)

Observing beauty in likely spots
Might be a healer when the summer's gone.
The food, too long in fridge, that brightly rots
Florescing may attractive hues take on.

Do you admire the rasp of creaking hinge?
Millay approves it—I have done the same.
Each bird astir, pre-vernal chirping binge
Has made for euphony a startling claim:

Some calls half-pitchless in the colloquy,
As in our conversation may occur,
Plus undetermined chirrings were to me
With caws well blent, for yearnings they aver.

A Messiaenic messaging they spawn,
Outspreading lessons on the thawing lawn.

79. Satie. His occult peregrinations may shed light on the contemplative nostalgia he would appear to share with, for example, Górecki and Pärt.

80. Goedicke. The idea of musically evoking pages of a dead soldier's diary fascinated me.

81. Antheil. This composition gives me the jazz context for **36 Kirchner** and **37 Gershwin**.

82. Ginastera. Liner notes made clearer to me the twofold nature of this composer's distinct achievement: Hispanic rhythmic and melodic legacy intensely blended with avant garde Schoenberg-style tone rows.

83. Clara Schumann. You'll notice the joy of her voice-and-piano composition made me want to invoke Beethoven's "Ode to Joy"—Clara being the new "Tochter aus Elysium."

84. Campion. He comes to mind instantly, along with Gibbons and Doland, whenever I get nostalgic for the glory days of Elizabethan song. (I'm boldly writing the latter's name without the customary "w" to help with correct pronunciation. In Doland's lifetime, the name "Roland" was written "Rowland." A. L. Rowse, in *The Elizabethan Renaissance: The Cultural Achievement* (1972), even suspects the name had earlier been the Irish "Dolan from Dublin" (120). Also, unless we use the "Doland" reading, the composer's clever motto—*Semper Dowland, semper dolens* ("Ever Dowland, ever grieving")—won't deliver the enjoyable tone-play he wanted.)

Whenever a person a word song's inventing
(4/13/18)

Whenever a person a word song's inventing,
The cheer of the hearer's own heartbeat augmenting,
    A gift he'll have offered that I'll have received
    As token of one who in music believed.

Whoever with fiddle some dancing has started
And grace of St. Patrick's Day gladly imparted
    A deed has revealed that I'm taking to heart:
    For me have you done it, dear brother in art.

Wherever a person has furthered tradition
By sweetness of tune to encourage a mission
    That aims to revive the Shakespearean age
    When poet-composer was Orphean mage,

When Campion, Doland, and Gibbons were reigning
And canorous chanter the vanguard was gaining,
    Be sure, as you dance in your canticle spree,
    I'm *with* you and *of* you, who've done it for me.

85. W. F. Bach. I recall once playing a fine duet of his for two violins...

86. Wagner. He was nothing if not epic, and it proved a sheer delight to survey his instrumental highlights in our English equivalent or analogue to the meter of Homer: dactylic hexameter.

87. Schnabel. To write this poem while surveying the tonescape of the Schnabel sonata was like taking a hike over varied terrain with startling "picturesque" views to halt the traveler.

88. Ligeti. My first-ever experience of this powerful poet in tones.

89. Handel. We have already heard of him twice—in **18 Schoenberg** and **58 Beethoven.** I'd like to add a tribute to some of his brief cantatas:

With *Alles jauchzet, lacht* I arise to write
(6/5/17)

With *Alles jauchzet, lacht* I arise to write
While fountains, blinding, shine in the skiey light.
      The oboe and the voice are vying,
    Sportive adornment with joy allýing.

With *Singe, Gott zum Preise* the boyish dance
Will echoes of Davidian psalm enhance.
      The hill, the lamb in bliss are leaping:
    Dotted, the rhythms are fieldward sweeping.

The current-streams *der spielenden Wellen* wave:
In soothing mood they earth and the spirit lave.
      The song with instruments competing
    Offers the noontide a riant greeting.

False cadences, that seem to resolve but don't,
Lead mind, delighted, far from its weary wont,

Each air, that, giddy, soon we're lost in,
Made like a park in the Age of Austen.

In Handel's neo-classical parks we find
Surprises planned with care and with art designed:
They're built to suit the guided tourist,
Views "picturesque" are of all the purest.

We're startled, too, repeatedly by the sound
*Da capo*s offer—improvisations found
Exuberant beyond all measure,
Bearing the legend *In Freedom, Pleasure.*

And here's what I wrote after a rehearsal of Handel's *The Messiah* with the Binghamton Community Singers, conducted by Kristi Ruffo (it was printed in the concert program):

Thoughts for Handel Singers
(9/20/17)

Ps. 24:7. Lift up your heads, O ye gates; and be ye lift up, ye everlasting doors; and the King of glory shall come in.
8. Who is this King of glory? The Lord strong and mighty, the Lord mighty in battle.
9. Lift up your heads, O ye gates; even lift them up, ye everlasting doors; and the King of glory shall come in.
10. Who is this King of glory? The Lord of hosts, he is the King of glory. Selah.

Lift up your heads, O ye gates!
How can a gate have a head?
Riddle solution awaits.
Think of a human instead.

You are the gate—it is you!
Let the Almighty come in!

Give Him a way to get through.
Then may the entry begin.

Folk bending over confine
Entryway into the chest.
Stand up erect! The Divine
Likes you, when highest, the best.

Lift up your eyes to a hill.
Quiet, breathe deeply. Then sing!
Ready His goal to fulfill,
Welcome the glorious King.

    To Handel was dedicated one of the first poems of my poet-life that started with retirement-retoolment 15 years ago:

Handel
(12/2/05)

*for Ruth Fisher, cellist and co-performer,
and for Suzanne Geoghegan, fundraiser event sponsor*

E major was the key of youth:
Audible apple-green or cloud-
less blue, a springtime power, proud
And glad and grand, allowed in truth

Progressions on the violin
Where sympathetic resonance
Of A and E string would enhance
A sharp and sprightly rising in

The work that spoke my fourteenth year
And shaped it as an anthem or
A story. Handel's gift was for
My heart to grow with. Happy, here,

Backed by the Susquehanna's green
And blue I play, again thirteen.

90. Rorem. Another first encounter for me, as with Ligeti and Schnabel. One feels that careful thought was devoted to the timbre, length, and placement of every note without exception.

91. Smetana. A highly painterly composition—visually rewarding thoughout. The theme of the "Moldau" section (about the Vltava River) circulated long and widely in eastern and central Europe; its originator is unknown.

And here's a bit of culture from Smetana-land in Binghamton NY:

Czecho-Slovak Mardi Gras
for Marianna DeCarlo
(2/29/12)

Waltz, polka—dancing—all you want!
But here's what most the folks may vaunt:
The cello, wailed with baleful cry,
They'll bury, gloomy faces gaunt.

Their hands they lay upon their friend
Whose days have hastened to an end,
While march funereal, with sigh
And Latin chant, will tribute send.

The "priest" brings holy water. It's
A bit of springtime slivovitz.
("They know their priests," with winking eye
A lady said—and wit that fits.)

He sprinkles drops on the deceased;
The heart of carnival, released,
Now gone, till Lent itself shall die
And fast give way again to feast.

92. Lalo. *Symphonie Espagnole,* like the *Symphonie Fantastique* of Berlioz, offers an experience of tonal storytelling on a wide scale, of melodious painting in broad compass.

93. Bloch. I am so grateful for this little gem! Years of listening to Bloch's *Schelomo*, his portrait of King Solomon for cello and orchestra, had prepared me well. And performing his *Suite Hébraïque* for violin and piano with Asher Raboy in a classical recital in Casadesus Hall at Binghamton University increased my love for the master.

94. Richard Strauss and **95. Berg.** In each response, I translate the lyric, a brilliant poem in itself. Then, thinking of the melody and rhythm both of the German lyric and of my own, I "translate" the total verbal-musical impression. I am in love with the delicate complexity of it all.

96. Balákirev. Compare this with **2 Moszkowski.**

97. Sibelius. Compare with the following evocation:

Sibelius' "Night Ride and Sunrise"
op. 55 London Symphony Antal Dorati
(10/10/9)

Confounding, unresolved, and wandering through dark,
The dotted rhythms unrelenting (that we heard
In *Grossë Fugë*) with a slipping of the wheels
In swifter groups intruding, still in minor key

The intimation of a village tune will mark
An alteration of the scene, a woodwind bird—
His intermittent punctuation—so one feels
A world awaking; varied instruments agree

As if the distant light relieved the somber stark
Monotony with landscape themes that heav'n preferred
To outline as it rose, the origin-ideals
Of home and morning ray the horns will hint to me,

Until the horses can relax, as in a park,
The duple time, erasing chaos that demurred,
Allowing choir-of-brass chorale that smooths and heals—
And violins are loosened, flying, hymning, free.

    98. Buxtehude. Here's an additional tribute to him:

Buxtehude's *Passion* you well might call it
(6/9/17)

Buxtehudë's *Passion* you well might call it—
Membra Jesu Nostri the rightful title:
Feet, knees, hands, side, chest, and the heart and face in
        Seven cantatas,

Holy madrigals of the sixteen eighties,
Each with prelude played by a viol consort.
Taught the grace of body-imagination,
        Hearing, the human

Learns a Bible passage, the Introduction,
Then relates the thought to a deed of mercy,
Dwelling on the empathy of the Savior,
        Martyr and mortal.

Ere the cloven side we in woe envision,
Solomonic word in a song will charm us:
Dove he calls to come from her hidden nest in
        Rock-hollow, wall-crack.

Ere to heart we turn for a clement refuge,
"You my heart have wounded, O spouse, O sister,"
In his hymn King Solomon our companion
        Begs for compassion.

Every kind of love we in Love are given
Let be shared—be sure they are brought together.

Every body part, when I pray, is praying;
　　　　Thanks, when I'm thankful.

99. Poulenc and Gervaise. I wrote the following about
the modern French composer:

Francis Poulenc
on a charcoal portrait of him by Aubrey Schwartz
(3/13/06)

He loved the winds and brasses. He enjoyed
Casual walking tempos, extraverted,
Brisk, and his wit was quick to be alerted
To music-mischief, pranks. True, he employed

Sound-blocks of organ chords, horns brooding, odd:
They're tragic moods that often quickly pass.
The tunes are singable. Gloria, Mass
Are homophonic, like a *promenade*

Such as he'll take in soft *concert champètre*
Or pastorale for oboe, clarinet,
Or woodwind work, elaborate sextet.
Relaxed *bel canto* is a *raison d'être...*

But thudding drums recall the rebels' rage
That guillotined the Carmelites offstage.

100. Purcell. Here is a quick sketch:

Henry Purcell
on a charcoal drawing of him by Aubrey Schwartz
(3/6/06)

You've likely heard more tunes by Púrcell than
You know—not only in the Britten young
Folk's guide to orchestra, but even sung
In *Beggar's Opera*; brash lyrics can

Conceal the context, not the melody
Found in the drama *Dioclesian* where,
As in the *Indian Queen*, a charming air
Will straightway captivate. For whether he

Is writing for the voice, or for the viol,
Recorder, shawm, or sackbut, clavichord—
Courant, or ayre, or hornpipe—he's a lord
Of limber English limpid singing. While

Queen Dido cries in fright (soon stilled in earth)
The famed *Rondeau* is yet a festive birth.

    I'll conclude these notes with a personal memory:

"Abdelazer" Ouverture and Dances
The Purcell Quartet, WSKG Binghamton NY
(6/22/11)

I played it as a twelve-year-old, and both
The suite and I have grown because the years
Have brought us each the phrasing-gift; who hears
The new performance, or my own, not loth

Will be to grant: They breathe it, feel the growth
And subsidence, the swell and ease, the troth
Of air and breast, the quiet that endears
At end of speaking, gentle to the ears.

The jig and minuet, the hornpipe, air,
The song "Lucinda Is Bewitching Fair,"
The tune that Britten borrowed, slighting, though,

Fine sections two and three of that rondeau—
I'm in the comfy metal folding chair...
Jane Hazelrigg conducts... I'm here, *I'm there*...

Index of Names

BOOKS OF ORIGINAL AND TRANSLATED VERSE
BY MARTIN BIDNEY

Series: East-West Bridge Builders

Volume I: *East-West Poetry:*
A Western Poet Responds to Islamic Tradition in Sonnets,
Hymns, and Songs
State University of New York Press

Volume II: J. W. von Goethe, *East-West Divan:*
The Poems, with "Notes and Essays": Goethe's
Intercultural Dialogues
(translation from the German with original
verse commentaries)
State University of New York Press

Volume III: *Poems of Wine and Tavern Romance:*
A Dialogue with the Persian Poet Hafiz
(translated from von Hammer's German versions,
with original verse commentaries)
State University of New York Press

Volume IV: *A Unifying Light: Lyrical Responses*
to the Qur'an
Dialogic Poetry Press

Volume V: *The Boundless and the Beating Heart*
Friedrich Rückert's The Wisdom of the Brahman
Books 1–4 in Verse Translation with Comment Poems
Dialogic Poetry Press

Volume VI: *God the All-Imaginer:*
Wisdom of Sufi Master Ibn Arabi in 99 Modern Sonnets
(with new translations of his Three Mystic Odes,
27 full-page calligraphies by Shahid Alam)
Dialogic Poetry Press

Volume VII: *Russia's World Traveler Poet:*
Eight Collections by Nikolay Gumilev:
Romantic Flowers, Pearls, Alien Sky, Quiver, Pyre,
Porcelain Pavilion, Tent, Fire Column
Translated with Foreword by Martin Bidney
Introduction and Illustrations by Marina Zalesski
Dialogic Poetry Press

Volume VIII: *Six Dialogic Poetry Chapbooks:*
Taxi Drivers, Magritte Paintings, Gallic Ballads,
Russian Loves, Kafka Reactions, Inferno Update
Dialogic Poetry Press

Volume IX: *A Lover's Art: The Song of Songs in Musical*
English Meters, plus 180 Original Love Poems in Reply—
A Dialogue with Scripture
Dialogic Poetry Press

Volume X: *A Hundred Villanelles, A Hundred Blogatelles*
Dialogic Poetry Press

Other Poetry Books by Martin Bidney

A Music Lover's Art: Wordsongs About Musical Compositions
Fourth Journal in Verse
Dialogic Poetry Press

Sufi Lyrics in the Egyptian Desert
Ninety Poems in Modified Omar Quatrain Form
Dialogic Poetry Press

The Rumi Interview Project: Ninety-nine Poems
from the Methnewi
Form-faithfully Translated from the Lyrical Versions
of Tholuck with Original Sonnet Replies
Dialogic Poetry Press

Book of the Dactyl: Third Journal in Verse
Including Poem-Dialogues with the Witty Mystic
Angelus Silesius
Dialogic Poetry Press

Book of the Anapest: Second Journal in Verse
A Feast of Word Song, with Notes
Dialogic Poetry Press

Book of the Amphibrach: First Journal in Verse—
A Feast of Word Song, with Notes
Dialogic Poetry Press

Book of the Floating Refrain: Tone-Crafted Poems
with Blogatelles
Dialogic Poetry Press

Bliss in Triple Rhythm—A Toolbox for Poets: Nine Ways to
Shape a Word Song Shown in 300 Original Poems
Dialogic Poetry Press

A Treat Not Known Before:
German-American Poetic Dialogues in Ancient Rhythms
Martin Bidney / Phlipp Restetzki
Dialogic Poetry Press

Rilke's Art of Metric Melody: Form-Faithful Translations with
Dialogic Verse Replies. Volume One:
New Poems I and II
Dialogic Poetry Press

A Hundred Artisanal Tonal Poems with Blogs
on Facing Pages:
Slimmed-down Fourteeners, Four-beat Lines,
and Tight, Sweet Harmonies
Dialogic Poetry Press

Shakespair: Sonnet Replies to the 154 Sonnets
of William Shakespeare
Dialogic Poetry Press

Alexander Pushkin, *Like a Fine Rug of Erivan:*
West-East Poems
(trilingual with audio, co-translated from Russian and
co-edited with Bidney's Introduction)
Mommsen Foundation / Global Scholarly Publications

Saul Tchernikhovsky, *Lyrical Tales and Poems of Jewish Life*
(translated from the Russian versions of Vladislav Khodasevich)
Keshet Press

A Poetic Dialogue with Adam Mickiewicz: The "Crimean Sonnets"
(translated from the Polish, with Sonnet Preface, Sonnet Replies, and Notes)
Bernstein-Verlag Bonn

Enrico Corsi and Francesca Gambino, *Divine Adventure: The Fantastic Travels of Dante*
(English verse rendition of the prose translation by Maria Vera Properzi-Altschuler)
Idea Publications [out of print]

Literary Criticism

Patterns of Epiphany: From Wordsworth to Tennyson, Pater, and Barrett Browning
Southern Illinois University Press

Blake and Goethe: Psychology, Ontology, Imagination
University of Missouri Press

[For e-books on Mickiewicz, Pushkin, and Bjerke
see martinbidney.org]